Strategy

1. Broadly 35-4
2. Repayable ove
3. Target rental
- Loan interest pr.
- Year 10 ie. when DR 63; oct 2022; ~~[illegible]~~ £10,000,000 COMM. prop. value

4 Purchasing:
.1 Identify 5-6 properties offer (if possible) 85-90% market value.
.2 All rents should be 10% + of value.
.3 Ideally a rolling 5 year plan - do not get into too much debt in case properties falling empty.
4. If available capital £500,000; then once this gone deposits to buy more Comm. Prop.

∴ "the plan". Sell all bus interests & concentrate on commercial property. - Need an office to work from!

5, Write a clear plan on how, who (legal advisers etc), accounts how it works; etc etc. Target date end of August; also visit Allsop auction; print off catalogues etc.

EASYWAY GUIDES

Managing Commercial Property

Steven Rimmer

Easyway Guides

Easyway Guides
Brighton BN2 4EG

British Library Cataloguing in Publication Data. A catalogue record for this book is available from the British Library.

ISBN 9781847161 12 3

Printed by GN Press Essex
Cover design by Straightforward Graphics

Whilst every effort has been taken to ensure that the information presented in this book is accurate at the time of going to print, the authors and publishers cannot accept any liability for errors or omissions contained within or for any changes to the law as it affects the management of commercial property.

Contents

Introduction

One major aspect of business that a business tenant/lessee enters into is that of signing an agreement for a business premises. This agreement may be a tenancy agreement, running from week to week or a longer-term lease running from 1year to 21 years (usually). The latter is known as a fixed term agreement and it is this type of agreement that is the main object of this book although periodic tenancies are referred to.

This book attempts to give a brief introduction to the effective management of business leases/tenancies of business premises. It is as comprehensive as possible, drawing on many years of experience and also taking aspects of management from best practice publications produced over the years. The approach is practical and seeks to avoid using technical jargon, allowing the business tenant, or prospective business tenant, to at least understand what it is they are signing up for.

To this end, the book begins by covering the nature of a lease and the way it is constructed, and then discusses specifically the nature of a business lease, covering rent reviews, maintenance, insurance, service charges (if applicable), assigning a lease, repossession, obligations under contract even when assigned, dispute resolution and security of tenure for business tenants under the law.

There are key points at the end of each chapter and there is a sample business lease in appendix 2.

1

Business Leases

This chapter deals generally with business leases and sets out the basic framework that governs these sorts of agreements. The fundamental principles of business leases are dealt with in the next chapter.

Many people entering into a business lease do not have a clear idea of what it is they are entering into. This is most often the case with those involved in setting up a business for the first time. The agreement signed with a landlord is, often, the single most expensive business item and it is potentially the area that will result in future problems if a clear understanding is not gained at the outset. Those new to business leases will find themselves confronted with a series of technical terms, some of which are interchangeable and are used throughout this book. These terms are as follows:

Lease or demise

A lease is a formal document under which land and premises is "demised" or leased to a tenant. Demised premises is a label for the land with a building or buildings.

Landlord or lessor

These alternative terms are used to describe the estate owner who grants the lease in question. A landlord can be a freeholder (outright owner) or head leaseholder.

Tenant or lessee

These interchangeable words describe a person who accepts a lease.

Assignor or assignee

By assignment is meant the outright transfer of the lease to another person. The assignor is the person transferring and the assignee the person accepting.

Sub leases (sub demises)

A sub lease takes place when a person already has a lease from a head landlord and that person creates another lease to someone else.

The relationship of the landlord to the leaseholder (tenant)

The relationship of the landlord to the tenant arises where one person who owns either the freehold or a leasehold interest in a property grants to another an interest which is lesser than his own term. The creation of a lease, correctly executed, passes a legal estate in land to the tenant. The lease must either be for a "term certain" or fixed term i.e. 5, 10 or 20 years, or for a periodic term, which runs from week to week or month to month and is capable of being ended by notice to quit from either party. On the termination of a fixed term lease or periodic tenancy, at the end of the term, the tenant's estate in land ends. However, the rules governing the ending of business leases are laid out clearly in the Landlord and Tenant Act 1954, Part 2, and unless a strict notice procedure prescribed by the Act is followed, then the lease will continue as a statutory tenancy. As we will see in Chapter 12, a business tenant has very clear rights to the continuation of a tenancy and the grant of a new tenancy unless the landlord has strong reasons for preventing this.

A lease, because it creates an estate in land, is much more than a mere personal or contractual agreement for the occupation of land by a tenant.

A lease confers a right in property, enabling the tenant to exclude all third parties including the landlord from possession for the duration of the lease, in return for the payment of rent.

A lease is distinct from a mere license to occupy, which confers no exclusive possession but merely gives the right to use a premises for strictly limited purposes.

If a written agreement for the occupation of any land or premises, whether residential or business contains three elements then it will be a lease or tenancy. These are:

(1) the grant of exclusive possession
(2) at a rent or for periodical payments
(3) for a fixed or periodic term.

It is not the intention to discuss further the distinction between license and tenancy. This book is intended for those who have signed a business tenancy/long lease and the above is for general guidance only.

The creation and the form of a business lease

A business lease is a conveyance in land and is as initially complex and time consuming (and expensive) as buying and selling any property. What seems simple on the face of it, especially for the frustrated would-be businessperson, who expects to come into possession of his or her property relatively quickly, is in reality a complicated process which has to be approached cautiously.

For the person entering into a business lease, there are three distinct stages in the overall transaction that it is important to be aware of:

- preliminary negotiations
- a contract or agreement for a lease
- The lease itself

Preliminary negotiations

This is the stage when the initial bargaining goes on, the property is inspected, the rent and other terms are discussed and references given on the part of the tenant. At this stage, either party remains free to withdraw under law. A contract is only concluded when the parties reach agreement on the granting of a lease. The role of agents in the process of negotiation will be discussed a little later in chapter two.

Contract for a lease

A contract for the leasing of land is not enforceable unless it is in writing. The prospective landlord promises that he will grant the lease and the prospective tenant promises that he will take the lease on the terms agreed. Finally, the lease is granted from this initial agreement and an estate in land is granted.

One general rule is that for an estate in land to be created it must be effected by deed. This deed will be incorporated within the document created as the lease and will contain the words "deed of grant". Another general, but important, rule, is that a lease must be in writing and witnessed to be enforceable in court. Again, the law surrounding this is complex and is beyond the scope of this book, suffice to say that the general principles mentioned above form the main body of the law.

The main terms of a lease

A business lease, in common with all leases, will contain the following main terms:

- The names of the parties, or their agents, or other sufficient description which will identify them. A general description will not usually suffice.
- The address of the property or a sufficient enough description to identify it.
- The term of the lease and the commencement date

- The rent and any premium for the premises. Quite often, in addition to rent, a premium, or one off payment, usually for "goodwill" will have to be paid.

- Landlord's covenants and tenants covenants. The meaning of covenants, which are basically undertakings, is discussed in greater detail below.

Most leases will contain standard clauses relating to repairing obligations, payment of rent, subletting and other general terms such as behaviour of tenant, overall use of the premises, assignment (transfer of lease) etc.

A lease and counterpart (duplicate) is usually prepared by the landlord's solicitor who will send the draft form of lease to the tenant's solicitor. The normal practice is for the tenant to bear all reasonable costs of the transaction. It is very important, if you are entering into a lease, to obtain quotes for the work beforehand and to get a clear idea of the overall coasts, including disbursements, such as stamp duty and land registration fees. All conveyances of land have to be registered with the land registry. Business leases will attract stamp duty, the amount of which can be checked with a solicitor.

Rights and obligations of parties under a lease

The rights and obligations of parties to any lease are governed by the *covenants* in the lease. There are three basic types of covenant:

- *Express covenants,* which regulate the exact nature and scope of each party's rights and obligations. These are discussed in greater depth further on.

- *Implied covenants.* These apply only so far as a lease fails to expressly provide for a matter but the implication on entering the contract is that a right or obligation exists

- *Statutorily implied covenants* which usually override the terms of the lease, the main principle being that statute overrides contract. Laws passed by Parliament and entered onto the statute form the basis of statutorily implied covenants.

All express covenants should be read clearly as these will form the framework for the relationship between landlord and tenant and, once entered into cannot be varied without either the agreement of the landlord or an order of court.

Examples of express covenants are those of rent, repairing obligations, insurance liabilities, use of premises, subletting and assignment. At common law, a tenant has the freedom to assign and any covenants to the contrary must be expressly imposed. As we will see a little later, a landlords consent to assignment cannot be unreasonably withheld. With business leases, the consent to assign is usually hedged with specific requirements relating to the premises in question, i.e., that the user will continue to use the premises for the use for which they are intended.

Rent and rent review within a lease

Rent is a contractual sum, which a landlord is entitled to receive at periodic intervals. Rent will be due even if the building is burnt down and the lessee cannot use the premises. A rent for the premises is agreed at the outset and this will normally be paid in advance, along with any service charges due for the premises (see chapter 6).

A rent review clause will usually be inserted into the lease and will normally be based on five-year review periods (depending of course on the length of the lease). The review clause is there to enable the landlord to receive rent which is a reflection of the market, thus maintaining the value of his or her investment. Rent reviews rarely result in rent reductions, usually the movement is upwards. The main elements of a rent review clause will be the periods of review, a formula for arriving at a market rent, any assumptions to be made about the premises such as the condition of the premises at the review date and the effect of any tenants improvements on the rent review (tenants improvements are generally ignored).

The rent review clause may contain procedures for the initiation of rent review by landlords notices, based on a given timetable.

Repairing obligations

Landlord and tenants repairing rights and obligations are expressly set out, or should be, in a lease. Usually, the tenant will assume full repairing and insurance liability on signing a lease. The landlord will usually have express covenants which will allow him or her to carry out repairs if needed, and carry out certain types of maintenance on a periodic basis, such as painting and associated repairs.

It is very important indeed that a would-be leaseholder takes full stock of repairing liabilities before signing a lease. This is to ensure that onerous repairing obligations are not assumed. For example, when taking on an assignment of a lease, it is essential that a survey of a property is carried out and that any future obligations are clear. Most leases will contain a covenant whereby on relinquishing a lease the tenant must make good any damage incurred during occupation, or restore the property to the condition it was in when first taken. This is generally based on a "schedule of dilapidations" produced by the landlord or the agent. It cannot be stressed enough that particular care must be taken when taking on the lease of a business premises. Repairs and maintenance can be an ongoing headache.

We will be looking at rent reviews in business leases in more detail in chapter 3.

Use of premises subject to the lease

The lease will define the use to which premises can be put. However, this will also be determined by planning regulations affecting the building and an area. For example, a parade of shops will have a predetermined use and this will be rigidly defined. The relevant planning class is usually outlined in a lease.

Some business premises contain a mixture of commercial and residential (the flat above the shop). A lease will also contain strict provisions regulating the use of the residential area, usually stipulating no subletting of part and intending the user of the business premises to occupy the residence as a home. If you intend to let such a premises then it is very important that you are clear about the uses to which the whole premises can be put.

Appendix 2 shows an example lease for a typical mixed commercial/residential premises.

****

Main points from chapter one.

- It is very important that a clear understanding of a business lease is gained at the outset. The lease should be read and any questions answered before entering into it.
- The creation of a business lease creates a legal interest in land
- The creation of a lease will entail preliminary negotiations prior to entering into the lease, the formation of a contract or agreement for a lease and the signing of the lease.
- Leases contain standard clauses called covenants, which outline the rights and obligations of landlord and tenant. Covenants can be express, implied or statutorily implied.
- It is very important indeed that landlord and tenant have a clear mutual understanding of rent and rent review clauses in the lease, and the mechanism for rent review.

2

Main Principles of Business Leases

In chapter one, we discussed leases generally and the construction of leases, pointing out the various rights and obligations of landlord and tenant. In this chapter, we will dwell more specifically on commercial leases.

The operation of business leases takes place within a complex legal framework which, if landlord and tenant are to manage effectively, has to be understood. In addition, agents should be employed to advise on those matters which are quite often outside the realms of the laypersons knowledge.

The role of advisors when negotiating a business tenancy

Legal advice concerning a lease is normally obtained from a solicitor experienced in property law. Solicitors will usually always be instructed to act on behalf of landlord and tenant. Surveyors and licensed conveyancers can also advise on property related matters. The extent of the advice will depend on the knowledge base of the advisor used and the complexity of the transaction.

The solicitor and client should discuss how the lease terms, and associated conditions, relate to the clients long-term needs. For example, is the length of lease adequate for the tenant's likely needs and whether the offered terms will enable a transfer of the lease to someone else. In addition, it may be that the client will want to make alterations to the premises to suit his or her business. The solicitor will advise on whether the lease allows this.

With some exceptions, the lease will be initially prepared by the landlord's solicitor who will pass it on to the client's advisor. Regardless, in the first instance, of whether the solicitor is acting for the landlord or tenant, the wording of the lease should reflect, as closely as possible, the client's requirements. If this cannot be achieved in important parts of the document then this should be pointed out to the client, along with the likely consequences.

In addition to the lease, the solicitor acting for the tenant will carry out certain checks to establish that the landlord owns the land and the buildings and enjoys rights of access. The solicitor will also check out certain matters with the local authority including the existence of any statutory notices, road schemes and other potential problems that they may know about. The conveyancing of a business lease from one to another has a lot of similarities to the conveyancing of any property, whether residential or business.

Solicitors are experts in their own chosen field and are not usually expert in the valuation of property or the physical aspects of buildings. They cannot advise on matters such as the correct level of rent, the complexities of rent reviews or other matters, which are properly the domain of a surveyor or other professional advisors.

Property advisors

Some property advisors have no formal qualifications and are not recognised by any professional body. You are well advised to avoid such advisors. This is mainly because of professional liability in the event of advice, which causes a business tenant to suffer later loss. The two main recognised professional bodies are:The Royal Institute of Chartered Surveyors (RICS) and The Incorporated Society of Valuers and Auctioneers (ISVA). Members of these professional bodies are property experts who are bound by strict rules of conduct laid down by these institutes. To become a member of either of the above, a practitioner has to spend many years initially qualifying and then has to develop knowledge on an ongoing basis throughout his or her career. In addition, professional indemnity cover, in case of loss through negligent advice, has to be maintained.

A property professional will be able to advise the tenant whether the rent being charged for premises, and service charge if appropriate, is reasonable and will be able to offer crucial advice concerning the relationship between the tenants needs and the lease terms. In addition, advice can be given on the condition of the building and any liabilities that the tenant is faced with over the longer term.

An effective business lease

As we have seen, a business lease is a very important document, which can restrict the tenant's freedom of action and prove detrimental to him or her over the longer term. Because of this, advice concerning the nature of the lease and how it is suited to the client's personal needs is of the utmost importance. As much as possible a lease should:

- Be readily understandable to the layperson. This means written in clear and plain English. Too often leases are couched in jargon, which is virtually incomprehensible and outdated in relation to the language used nowadays.
- A lease should be concise and relevant, avoiding long windedness and irrelevancies.
- A lease should be linked from one section to another, with any schedules clearly linked to the relevant sections. As we have seen, a lease is constructed of various component parts and should, overall, represent a cohesive whole to the reader. The ultimate test is whether a layperson can gain a clear idea of exactly what are the rights and obligations of each party to the lease, before having to resort to obtaining legal advice.
- The lease should state clearly any legal position relevant to the transaction, such as certain consents not being unreasonably withheld although statute clearly states this. This is because, as much as anything else, a lease should be an educative document, which attempts to enlighten those who become party to it and does not attempt to obscure or conceal.

It is the case that many leases are reproductions of previous leases and still fall short of the mark in being clear, concise and educative. However, there are model leases in existence, in particular the one produced by the law society, which attempt to serve as models of leases to be used in business transactions. Although they may not suit all types of transaction, they serve as useful models when attempting to achieve clarity.

Negotiating a business lease

When considering entering into a business lease, it should be remembered that all the terms within the lease are negotiable. However, as with all negotiations the extent to which terms are negotiable is determined by a number of factors. These are:

- The background of competition. Obviously, the situation of supply and demand at any one particular moment will affect the power of individuals involved in the transaction. Rent, for example, will be determined by the ability of the would-be lessee to go elsewhere if the price is not suitable.

- The particular circumstances of the landlord and tenant will have a bearing on the negotiations. Very much will depend on the position of each in relation to their willingness to concede to the others demands.

- The financial standing of the tenant. This will influence the negotiations in that the more economically powerful the tenant, the more that the landlord may be willing to concede to demands if it is perceived that that person (or company) is a "blue chip' tenant.

The overall effect of the above is that the flexibility of lease terms will tend to vary depending on time, place and circumstance. When considering taking on a business lease, therefore, the would-be tenant should consult a property advisor in order to ascertain his or her position and to gain an idea of the landlord's objectives in negotiating the lease and to check that the terms reflect market conditions.

Landlords should be flexible when faced with a request to alter a particular term of the lease. Although this may result in a compromise having to be made it will also result in a situation in which the landlord is perceived as being fair. Both parties to the lease, and their advisors, should explore fully what terms are negotiable and become fully acquainted with market conditions.

In addition, the landlord should be open to initial requests for a rent-free period to allow alterations to the premises to take place. During these alterations trading may be impossible, resulting in a loss of revenue. Both landlord and tenant should be able to meet in the middle and reach a compromise during this crucial period. It should be expected that if it takes a tenant one-month to fit out and another two weeks to commence trading then a two-month rent-free period should be allowed as reasonable. In times of supply exceeding demand, situations exist where rent-free periods are automatically offered as an incentive.

It has to be remembered that the relationship between landlord and tenant continues after the lease has been signed and it is very important that the interaction between parties is flexible and constructive. When either party proposes to take action which is likely to have significant consequences for the other, the party proposing the action should notify the other of the intended action and the consequences. Examples of action could be rent review, planning applications, imminent redevelopment and changes in the provision of services. Many leases specify time limits to be followed and details of particular steps.

****

Main points from chapter 2

- The operation of business leases takes place within a complex legal framework which needs to be understood by landlord and tenant.
- Advice concerning both the nature of the lease and also property matters should be obtained from expert advisors.
- It is essential that those from whom advice is sought are members of recognized professional bodies.
- The effective business lease has to be readily understandable to the layperson, be concise, relevant and free of irrelevancies.
- All the terms of a business lease are negotiable in the first instance. This is a very important stage as, once entered into, the lease is binding.
- It may be possible to negotiate a rent-free period at the outset of a lease in order to set up the business. This will depend on a number of market related factors.

3

Rent Reviews

As mentioned in chapter one, leases, in particular business leases, will contain provisions for rent reviews at specified intervals. In business leases of a longer term it is usual for this period to be every five years. This will normally be based on a formula and will inevitably involve an increase in rent.

Before discussing rent reviews, it is important that the business tenant understands the basis for arriving at an initial rent, should have done some initial basic research and understands the frequency of payment. In addition, the tenant should read and understand the basis for any other charges made under the lease, such as service charges. If the business premises are part of a bigger building with other premises then it is likely that a service charge will be made for the upkeep of common parts and any communal repairs deemed necessary. Sometimes, a sinking fund will be allowed for, which enables the managers to ensure that money is available for longer-term major repairs.

The lease will usually contain detailed provisions relating to service charges and these are discussed in more depth in chapter 6. It is also important that the consequences of non-payment of rent are understood. Usually, non-payment of rent on a given date will result in the charging of interest on monies not paid. Depending on the managing agent this either will or will not be levied. It is important to alert the owner or agent to the possibility of late or delayed payments in order to avoid bad feeling and possible legal action.

Rent reviews

A new rent for a property is more likely to be the letting value of a property in the open market at the time of rent review. The exercise involves looking at comparables in the area and drawing comparisons before arriving at a rental figure.

While it is usual for a rent to be agreed, assuming that an open market rent is easily calculated, it is absolutely essential that a clause be inserted in the lease which tells either party how the rent will be arrived at in the event of disagreement. Solicitors or property advisors should be able to advise on the nature and extent of arbitration should an agreement not be reached. Sometimes, an independent expert will be provided for, otherwise alternative dispute resolution should be considered. This will be discussed in more detail in chapter 10.

The following are examples of the ways that rent can be revised:

- *Upwards only.* This means that the rent will either be increased or will stay the same. It cannot be reduced. This is called an "Upwards Only" clause.
- *Minimum base rent.* The rent cannot fall below the rent first payable at the beginning of the lease but subject to that can go

up or down depending on the market value at the time of the review.

- *Open Market Value.* The rent will simply be subject to market forces at the time of review and can therefore go up or down.
- *Turnover rent.* A turnover rent is normally either a combination of a base rent and an element reflecting a tenant's turnover, or a simple percentage of turnover.
- *Index linked.* This means that the rent review, and subsequent increase will be linked to a given index, such as the Retail Price Index.
- *Fixed increases.* In this case the lease will simply state when and by how much the rent will be increased.

It is very important that the prospective tenant is clear about rent and rent reviews before taking on a lease. Property advisors will usually give a considered opinion. However, questions such as "how much will the rent be in five years time" are impossible to answer as, unless there is a specific clause in a lease concerning rental increase then market forces will always prevail.

****

Main points from chapter 3.

- Business leases usually contain a rent review clause allowing for a rent increase after a period of time. This clause can be presented in a number of ways. Usually, the review will result in an increase of rent.

- A new rent for a property is more likely to be the letting value of the property in the open market at the time of the rent review.

4

Maintenance Obligations

The obligation to carry out repairs under a lease will vary. However, there is a main principle and that is that, notwithstanding whose responsibility it is to actually carry out the repairs, the tenant will always pay. This will either be by way of a direct payment or through service charges.

Directly related to the above principle, some leases are referred to as *full repairing and insurance leases.* In addition to repairs, the tenant is liable for insurance costs.

Where there are several tenants, each will normally be responsible for the internal repair of their part of the premises and for contributing towards the landlord's costs of maintaining the exterior, structure and common parts.

Given that repairs and maintenance to a property will vary according to the state of the property and the attitude of the landlord, it is very advisable for a prospective tenant to instruct a chartered surveyor to undertake a survey of the premises.

This will help with negotiating and assessing the implications of the repairing obligations, which are to apply at the beginning, during and at the end of the lease. (See appendix 2 – sample business lease)

The lease, or a supplementary agreement may include a record of the survey, together with photographic evidence of condition (called a schedule of condition) which may, with the agreement of individuals provide a benchmark for future repair work. This will also enable the tenant to work out likely outgoings over the course of the lease.

The ability of the tenant to carry out a survey will generally be dictated by the size of the building. In larger buildings it is impractical to carry out a survey and the overall maintenance will be, or should be, managed through a service charge. It is essential for a prospective tenant to understand the framework governing the collection and use of service charges. This is discussed further in chapter 6. .

Towards the end of the lease term, notwithstanding the tenants attitude towards renewal (see chapter 12 "Right to renew") the landlord will normally serve a notice on the tenant requiring the tenant to carry out certain repairs to bring the building back up to the standard of the original at the time of taking on the lease. This is called a "schedule of dilapidation's" It is very common for there to be disagreement over these, particularly where the management during the lease term has been lax and virtually no repairs have been carried out. The effect of this is that repairs have been stored up and there will be heavy expenditure at the end.

Landlords vary, and their skill, ability and attitudes will also vary. So will the attitudes of any managing agents employed. It is very important and advisable to obtain professional opinion if faced with a schedule of dilapidation's that you disagree with. The costs of employing a professional advisor may be more than offset by the savings achieved on any repairs demanded.

The ultimate goal of landlord and tenant is to manage in an efficient manner during the course of the lease and to ensure that expenditure on repairs and maintenance is even throughout the lease term. The worse scenario and the most problematic is trying to put a badly maintained building back to rights.

****

Main points from chapter 4

- Obligations to carry out repairs under a lease will vary. However, the general principle is that, notwithstanding who carries out the repairs the onus will be on the business tenant to pay for the work.

- It is very important at the outset to prepare a property schedule which will enable you to gain an idea of ongoing repair bills and also to negotiate with the landlord at the end of the lease.

5

Insurance

The terms of a business lease will vary in relation to the provision of insurance. However, in much the same way as repairing obligations, there is one main principle. Regardless of who arranges the insurance, the tenant will pay the premiums.

The main form of insurance for a premises is usually buildings insurance, which will pay for any identified insurable risks, ranging from fire to flood damage, from partial damage to outright destruction. Many policies will not cater for "Acts of God" such as earthquake. However, there are relatively few earthquakes in Britain so this is not a real problem. In addition to buildings insurance, there will always be a requirement for public liability insurance, which will usually be arranged by the tenant.

In addition to these two main forms of insurance a tenant may be required under a lease to provide insurance for plate glass, if relevant in the event of window breakage. Even if this is not required the tenant should consider getting adequate cover as the cost of replacing broken windows can be prohibitive. The premium will vary depending on the location of the shop. If the premises are situated next to a notorious pub then it is likely that an insurer will charge more than if the shop was tucked away in a little side street.

In relation to buildings insurance, if the tenancy is of new-build premises, the role of insurance is crucial, as a distinction needs to be made between the insurers liabilities and developer's liabilities. Normally, the managing agents or the owner would be taking charge of this area.

Sometimes the lease will give the landlord or the tenant the right to end the lease if the premises are very badly damaged, rather than reinstate them. Where the damage is insured there may be important questions about how, why and by whom the insurance money is spent and the parties will need to take professional advice at the outset.

Tenants should consider taking out their own insurance in respect of loss or damage of contents. Obviously, if a lot of time and money has been spent fitting out a shop and there is a break-in then the presence of a comprehensive insurance policy will go a long way to rectifying the situation and to enable the tenant to begin trading as soon as possible. Insurance can also be taken out to cover loss of profits.

Tenants should check that the provisions for suspension of rent following insured damage are either indefinite or sufficiently long to enable the reinstatement of the building to take place.

It is a fact that, as with household insurance, many of those involved in business will not take out adequate insurance cover in order to save on money and reduce outgoings. However, as we have discussed, certain insurances are a requirement of the lease, such as buildings insurance and public liability insurance. The other insurance's, such as contents, loss of profits and damage to plate glass are essential and should not be ignored. At the outset they should be factored in as a cost.

It is also essential that a business tenant has a copy of the insurance policy in force and understands the full extent of cover. There are quite often incidences where the tenant will pay out unnecessarily for works which are insurable.

****

Main points from chapter 5

- The terms of a business lease will vary in relation to the provision of insurance. Regardless of whose responsibility it is to provide the insurance, it will usually be the tenant's responsibility to pay.

- Insurance for premises will normally consist of buildings insurance and public liability insurance. However, the lease may require the provision of other forms of insurance, such as the protection of plate glass. It is essential to ensure that necessary insurance is in place.

6

Service Charges

Although there is comprehensive provision for residential properties, principally flats, for service charges, under the Landlord and Tenant Acts 1985/1987 and 1996, plus the 2002 Commonhold and Leasehold Reform Act, the Act do not apply to business premises.

The framework that applies to residential properties however, forms the basis of good practice for the delivery of services, the charging and the accounting for services to business premises.

Service charges, normally levied when 2 or more business units are joined, are those charges over and above the rent charged for a property. Rent usually provides a profit to the owner and will not cover any additional costs associated with the upkeep of the property, such as the reasonable costs of repair, maintenance and replacement of the fabric, plant and equipment and materials necessary for the property. In addition there will be common parts, which will need to be heated and adequately lit and gardens and other amenity areas, which need to be serviced.

Another charge, which may be included in a service charge, will be that of longer-term major repairs or replacements. This will have to be justified by the landlord as not many business tenants like their money being tied up in this way.

Sometimes, staff will need to be employed, particularly if the unit is part of a larger retailing center and these costs will be passed on, along with any ongoing contracts to maintain and repair plant and equipment, such as lifts and escalators.

The landlord may wish to charge insurance through the service charge and will also usually charge an administration fee to cover the costs of staff time in managing services. This will normally be about 10% of the overall costs of services.

Service charge costs should not otherwise include:

a) any initial capital costs incurred in relation to the original design and construction of the fabric of the building, plant or equipment
b) any setting up costs which are reasonably to be considered as part of the original development cost of the property.
c) Capital improvement costs above the costs of normal maintenance, repair or replacement.
d) future redevelopment costs
e) such costs as are matters between the owner and an individual occupier via enforcement's of covenants for collection of rent, costs of letting units, consents for assignments, sub-letting, alterations, rent reviews etc.

Ultimately, one of the fundamental principles underpinning provision for services is that the services should be relevant and beneficial to the needs of the property, the owner, the tenant and the customers. Excessive profits should not be made and all costs should be accounted for. A budget should be produced for consultation about three months prior to the start of the financial year.

Value for money

Disputes about service charges, whether residential or business property, are frequent, long, drawn out and expensive and the management of charges is always under scrutiny. Therefore, it is essential that value for money is achieved.

Service quality should be appropriate to the location, age, use and character of the property. The owner should seek to achieve that service quality as cost effectively as possible, costs should be kept under review and, where appropriate, contractors and suppliers should be regularly required to submit competitive tenders or to provide competing quotations.

Contractors and suppliers of services should be required to perform to written performance standards agreed with the owners and tenants.

Service charge apportionments

Another fundamental principle of service charge management is that of fair apportionment. This is undoubtedly one of the most difficult areas to get right. Leases will normally spell out the basis for apportionment, and the formula will be arrived at depending on the number of properties, their position in relation to the consumption of individual services and the nature of the overall property.

Service charges will usually be apportioned through the use of percentages or by a straight division, whichever is the more equitable. For example, if a shopping center is on three floors, is it fair that the ground floor pays for lift depreciation, annual maintenance contracts and wear and tear of escalators? The answer would probably be yes because shoppers take advantage of the whole site and all ultimately benefit. It is usually easier to divide by the straight-line method in which all pay equally.

Taking on board the above, the following key principles of apportionment should apply:

- Apportionment of costs to each occupier should be on a fair and reasonable basis, in accordance with the principles of good estate management and applied fairly and consistently throughout the property having regard to the physical size, nature of use and the benefit to the occupier or occupiers.

- The occupiers should not be charged through the service charge or otherwise collectively towards costs attributable to unlet premises. Also, the cost of a special concession by an owner to any one occupier should be met by the owner.

- The owner should bear a fair proportion of the costs attributable to his use of the property, e.g. where a center management suite is used in part as an owners regional office.

- If the property is fully let the owner should normally be able to recover all expenditure on services through the service charges.

- The estimated budget of service charge expenditure and certificated accounts should set out the method used to determine each occupiers share of the costs.

The above are a few of the key considerations when looking at apportionment of charges to business tenants.

Consultation with business users

The Landlord and Tenant Act 1985 (as amended) sets out a rigorous framework for consultation for residential occupiers of flats. This lays down a framework within which landlords must consult when expenditure is over a certain limit and also prescribes a time period and the need to supply estimates and allow feedback.

There is no such legislative requirement for business premises. However, the principles underlying the 1985 Act (as amended) inform the spirit of good practice underlying service charge provision to commercial premises.

Effective managers will always realize that communication between managers and tenants is essential to arrive at consensus. If large amounts of money are to be spent or there is to be a change in services and the cost of services then adequate notice should be given to tenants to allow them to voice opinion. If the work is costly then several estimates should be obtained and these sent to tenants and their opinion sought.

Although there is no formal legal framework governing the provision of services to commercial property there is always the ***lease*** *which will serve as the main document in any dispute. Ultimately, the tenant can always sue in the county court, alleging breach of contract or general inequity.*

Estimated budget expenditure

As with all service charges, whether residential or business, an estimate of expenditure for the forthcoming year has to be produced, in order to give tenants the opportunity to feed back and, if necessary, object to the forthcoming charges.

The budget will always coincide with the financial year of the organization or individual in question. If significant charges are made then this will be stipulated in the lease. If, for example, the financial year begins on the 1st April each year, ending on the 31st March the next year then the budget for the forthcoming year should be presented at the latest by the beginning of February, to business tenants.

The budget should be broken down into individual heads of charge and be in a consistent format from year to year. The individual occupiers share of expenditure should be clearly set out in the budget. Explanation should be provided if there is a significant variation of costs over the previous year and also the previous years accounts should be laid out alongside the anticipated expenditure in order for the tenant to be able to interpret information.

Normally, and depending of course on the size of a scheme, a meeting will be held several months before the start of the financial year in order to discuss charges and answer any questions. This is seen as good practice and essential if good relations are to be maintained with tenants. If a letter and the figures are sent out to tenants without a prior meeting, it is likely that a lot of time will be spent dealing with queries.

The provision of certified accounts

The lease will normally outline the framework for the preparation of certified accounts and the provision of such to tenants. The Landlord and Tenant Acts 1985/1987 (as amended) lay down the requirements for residential leaseholders. The spirit of the Act flows through the principles and practice of commercial property management. The following summarises good practice:

- The owner should normally submit certified accounts to the occupiers in a timely manner and, in any event, within six months of the year-end (end of service charge year).

- The accounts should give a reasonably comprehensive level of detail to enable occupiers to compare expenditure against estimated budget. Given the difference between the outlook of the financial professions and the average person, it is also very wise indeed to send out a management letter to tenants, which elaborates on each head of expenditure and explains any marked differences.

- The owner should allow occupiers a reasonable time to feed back on the accounts and to raise queries.

- Owners should deal with reasonable enquiries in a prompt and efficient manner and make relevant documentation available for inspection. It is usual for tenants to wish to see invoices for the year in question. Where copies are made available, a reasonable fee may be charged.

- An auditor should certify the accounts, with the costs charged to the service charge accounts. If an occupier requests his own audit, the owner should agree and the audit fee charged to the occupier.

It is good practice, as with budgets, to hold a meeting to discuss audited accounts. A letter reaching business users, even with a management letter can result in so much confusion that solicitors can be employed to deal with the query, which again results in valuable time being eaten up and ill feeling created. Nothing can replace initial face-to-face communication, followed by prompt action with regard to queries.

Sinking funds

As mentioned previously, sometimes it is prudent, and necessary, to charge a sinking fund, which is designed to cater for longer-term maintenance and replacement of items. This will build up in an interest bearing account. The fund should be built up on the basis of a plan, usually based on a survey of the building and associated components, such as lift replacements.

The Landlord and Tenant Acts 1985/1987 (as amended) regulate the use of monies placed in a sinking fund for residential properties. This act requires that money be placed on trust for the tenants so that it is not affected by any actions against the owner, such as liquidation. In addition, there are clear requirements that it should be accounted for.

The same principles will apply to commercial properties. Good practice dictates that and money raised for longer term repairs, such as cyclical redecoration and repairs, and also replacements of capital items and major repairs to the building, along with any funds designed to replace furnishings and floor coverings, should be separated out into interest bearing client accounts, or trust accounts, separate from the owners own monies.

The management of service charges is an extremely important area and is also an area prone to litigation. It is also usually an area, particularly in larger retail centers, that is normally undertaken by professionals. In smaller premises, it will normally be undertaken by a managing agent or an owner, but the same rigorous principles should apply.

****

Main points from chapter 6

- The framework governing the provision of service premises will usually be set out in the lease. It is essential that this is clearly understood as service charges constitute an additional expense, on top of rent.

- Service charges are normally to be found where a number of business premises are adjoined, such as a shopping centre and it is essential for the landlord to provide services to the premises in order to enable them to function efficiently.

- One of the fundamental principles underpinning the provision of services to commercial property is that the services should be relevant and beneficial to customers.

- Landlords should aim to provide value for money and should provide budgets well in advance of the start of a financial year and accounts within six months of the year-end.

- Apportionment of services should accurately reflect the service received by the tenant.

- It is of the utmost importance that business tenants and landlords engage in the process of face-to-face consultation concerning expenditure, particularly on larger items.

7

Assignment and Sub-letting

One of the main principles underlying the purchase of a leasehold interest in land is that the leaseholder has the right, generally subject to the permission of the landlord, which cannot unreasonably be withheld, to assign (pass on, through sale usually or can be paying someone to take on the lease) or sublet the premises (whole not part).

The subletting of a premises means the granting of a sublease, under the same terms and conditions, to someone else.

There will normally be a restriction, to some extent, on the lessee's right to assign or sublet or share the premises. The assignment of only part of the premises is usually prohibited.

Often the lease provides that the tenant has to obtain the landlords consent to assign or sublet. The consent will usually depend on the potential assignee passing some form of test by meeting certain criteria. In some cases, the test takes the form of the landlord exercising some form of subjective judgment and in most of these cases the landlords consent cannot be unreasonably withheld and the landlord cannot demand money as a condition of getting it. In other cases the landlord will have set objective tests which simply have to be met, the landlord exercising no discretion.

The legal framework regulating the landlords and tenants actions is the 1988 Landlord and Tenant Act, which imposes the following duties on the landlord:
"Where the tenant serves on the landlord or other person who may consent, a notice to assign, the landlord owes the tenant a duty, within a reasonable time:

a) to give consent, except where it is not reasonable to do so;

b) to serve on the tenant written notice of his decision, whether or not he gives consent.

Where a notice is served, it must specify any conditions attached to consent, or the reasons for withholding it, as the case may be. The 1988 Act cannot be evaded by imposing an unreasonable condition to avoid giving consent.

If a landlord receives a written consent application, where, in addition to his own consent, the consent of a superior landlord is required as well, then the recipient is bound to take reasonable steps to secure the receipt within a reasonable time of a copy of the application by that person.

A landlord or superior landlord who is under the above duties must show, if challenged by the tenant, that he gave consent within a reasonable time. Likewise, the onus is on a landlord or superior landlord to show that any condition is reasonable, where the 1988 Act applies, and if consent is refused then the onus is on the landlord to show that refusal was reasonable.

The following general principles govern the question of whether refusal was reasonable:

- A landlord is not entitled to refuse consent to an assignment on grounds which have nothing to do with the relationship of landlord and tenant in regard to the subject matter of the particular demise of the premises, such as an alleged difficulty in re-letting other premises.
- If the landlord refuses consent to a proposed assignment or sub-letting because of general reasons of good estate management relating to the whole building, not the particular part let to the tenant, the refusal will be unreasonable.
- It is not necessary for the landlord to prove that the conclusions which led him to refuse consent were justified, if they were conclusions reasonably reached in the circumstances.
- It may be reasonable for a landlord to refuse consent to a proposed assignment on the ground of the purpose for which the assignee wishes to use the premises, even though that purpose is not forbidden by the terms of the lease.

Examples of reasonable withholding of consent

A landlords reasonable withholding of consent has been held to be reasonable where the landlord believed that the proposed assignee or sub tenant was objectionable for some personal or financial reasons, or that the future earnings or financial viability of the property would be endangered. In addition, a landlord supplied with insufficient information, for example in reference or in accounts, is entitled to withhold consent.

Examples of unreasonable withholding of consent

A refusal of consent is unreasonable where the sole reason is to gain possession, or where the reason is not bona fide, or where the tenant is in breach of repairing covenants and the assignee is prepared to spend a considerable sum on executing repairs. It is not possible to withhold consent on the grounds of race or sex. Generally, it is not possible to withhold consent for reasons outside of the lease.

Remedies for withholding consent

If a tenant is advised that a refusal of consent is unreasonable, or that unreasonable conditions have been imposed on the giving of consent, the tenant can carry out the transaction concerned, risking forfeiture of the lease (loss of lease). The tenant may alternatively apply to the court, usually the county court, for a declaration that the refusal was unreasonable.

Where the Landlord and Tenant Act applies and the landlord unreasonably refuses consent, or is deemed to have done so, the tenant may claim damages from the landlord, and any superior landlord.

Remedies of landlord

The landlord may, if he or she could have reasonably withheld consent, provided the lease entitles him to, bring an action to forfeit the lease. If in forfeiture proceedings, the court rules that the landlord could not have unreasonably withheld his consent, it has the discretion to grant relief from forfeiture.

****

Main points from chapter 7

- One of the main principles underlying the purchase of a leasehold interest in land is that the leaseholder has the right, generally subject to the permission of the landlord, which cannot unreasonably be withheld, to assign a lease or to sublet the whole of the premises.
- The restrictions placed on assignment or subletting will normally be those of the suitability of the proposed assignee and a number of criteria will usually be outlined in the lease which will form the basis of a test.
- The legal framework regulating the actions of the landlord and tenant is the 1988 Landlord and Tenant Act.
- A landlord is not allowed to refuse consent to assign on grounds which have nothing to do with landlord and tenant.
- A business tenant can apply to a county court to review a landlords decision if he or she think that it is unreasonable.

8

Repossession of a Business Lease by The Landlord

When a landlord and tenant enter into a lease, there is a duty by both to observe covenants under the lease. As we have seen, these can be express, implied or statutorily implied covenants. They will bind tenants to pay rent, keep the premises in good repair, pay service charges, not to carry out any alterations, not to cause a nuisance and, usually, not to assign or sublet without the landlords consent. In addition, there is a binding covenant not to sublet part. These are some of the main tenant's covenants.

The landlord will also be under a duty to observe covenants in the lease, to allow quiet enjoyment and to observe particular repairing covenants, amongst others.

There are remedies for both parties when either side does not observe the covenants. If a tenant feels that a landlords covenant is not being observed then legal advice will be needed before taking any kind of action.

Often, it is the tenant who is faced with repossession and it is the ultimate sanction of repossession which will be outlined below.

A lease will contain a clause, called a forfeiture clause, giving the landlord the right to re-enter, i.e. re-possess the property if the tenant fails to pay the rent within a fixed period (usually 21 days) after the due date, or breaks any of the other obligations or becomes insolvent.

However, the landlord does not simply have the right to re-enter a premises. If the landlord wishes to evoke the forfeiture clause, a strict notice procedure must be observed and a court hearing obtained. Until the process has been gone through by the landlord then the tenant has security of tenure. Any unlawful attempts to evict will result in a damages claim against the landlord.

If a business tenant is faced with the threat of forfeiture then immediate legal advice will be needed, as this is a complicated area and the business tenant has a series of protections before a premises can be repossessed.

****

Main points from chapter 8

- When a landlord and tenant enter into a lease, both have a duty to observe covenants under the lease. Breach of covenant can lead to court action to remedy the breach.

- Breach of covenant by the tenant can lead to forfeiture, or loss of the lease. This is a long, involved and costly process. Both landlord and tenant are advised to try to resolve disputes informally before any action.

- If a tenant has problems paying rent then it is advisable to contact the landlord as soon as possible in order to negotiate extra time and therefore avoid legal action.

9

Privity of Contract

There are a number of anomalies with a business lease leading to what tenants and advisors see as ultimate inequity. One such inequity is the principle of privity of contract.

Essentially, privity of contract means that, even if a lease is assigned to another, the original leaseholder will remain liable for any breaches of that lease, even if the breaches have been committed by the assignee. This can be particularly worrying when the person assigned to does not comply with the obligation to pay rent.

Such is the problem associated with privity of contract that rules have been introduced to ameliorate this. Leases granted before January 1996 are still subject to privity of contract but there are three important changes to simple liability:

- From 1st January 1996, although leases signed before this time are still subject to privity of contract, the potential liability is reduced in one respect – where the tenants liability has increased as a result of the landlord exercising an absolute discretion to permit a change to the lease (for example, the landlord has permitted a change of use which has resulted in an increase in rent) then the former tenant will not be liable for that element of liability attributable to that change.

- The landlord must serve notice of any potential claim against a former tenant or former guarantor of rent, service charge, specified liquidated damage or interest within six months of the tenant's default. Failure to do so means that the landlord cannot recover that amount from the former tenant or guarantor.

- A former tenant or guarantor who pays such a claim will be able to require the landlord to grant him or her an overriding lease. This will enable the former tenant to reclaim control of the premises and to take action to mitigate any loss.

Leases granted on or after 1st January 1996 (without any previous commitment to take the lease)

Tenant privity of contract is abolished for these leases. However, an outgoing tenant can be required to guarantee its immediate assignee. The guarantor, however, can only cover the performance of the assignee and must end at the next assignment.

Landlord privity of contract can be brought to an end, but only if the tenant agrees or the court decides.

The three changes above also apply to these leases.

****

Main points from chapter 9

- One of the main principles guiding business leases is that of privity of contract. This is where a former lessee is responsible for any breaches of a lease by an assignee.

- From 1st January 1996, liability for any obligations under a previously held business lease is reduced.

- From 1st January 1996, under a new contract, liability for actions of an assignee cease to exist, although a landlord can require some form of guarantee from the outgoing tenant.

10

Disputes

Often, disputes will arise over one or more elements of the lease and landlord and tenant will have to work out a means of resolving these disputes. Usually, the lease, if well drafted, will contain a mechanism to resolve disputes before the courts intervene. This will often take the form of the appointment of a professional to arbitrate and reach a decision acceptable to both parties. However, if the lease contains no such mechanism then the courts will have to decide.

It is vital that both landlord and tenant have some idea of the nature of resolving disputes and the facts outlined below are designed to raise awareness of the nature and role of the arbitrator and expert and also the usefulness of informal procedures to avoid the costs associated with the use of professionals.

The two most commonly used alternatives to proceedings in the court are:

a) Arbitration
b) Decision by independent expert

One or other of these alternative procedures should be specified for rent reviews that cannot be agreed. They may also be used to settle other problems as well, for example, disputes about service charges or repairs. Awards by arbitrators and determinations by independent experts have some things in common, but in some respects they are different. The main points of comparison and differences between the two are as follows:

- Arbitrators and experts are appointed, in the first instance, by agreement between landlord and tenant.

- If an appointment cannot be agreed, an appointment is made by an independent person, usually the president of the Royal Institute of Chartered Surveyors.

- An arbitrator is professionally qualified in the subject matter of the dispute and skilled in arbitration law and procedure, whereas the expert is professionally qualified in the subject matter of the dispute with particular knowledge of the type of property and locality.

- An arbitrator is bound to decide the dispute according to the evidence submitted and is not entitled to carry out own investigations and research. The expert, on the other hand is expected to carry out own research. The expert can also disregard any evidence put forward by the landlord or tenant.

- The arbitrator is bound to conduct a hearing, at which both parties are present, if a meeting is requested. The expert need not hold any hearing.

- An arbitrator must conduct the arbitration in a fair and just manner. The expert must act with due care and diligence but is not bound by the principles of natural justice.

- The arbitrator must ensure that each side has details of the other side's case, and the opportunity to answer it in writing or orally at a hearing. An arbitrator will usually give directions at the beginning of a meeting as to how this is to be achieved. The expert has discretion as to whether there should be procedures for the disclosure and rebuttal of any special case advanced by landlord and tenant.

- The arbitrator can order one side or the other to pay all or part of his and the opposing sides costs. The expert cannot order costs unless the lease provides for this.

- The arbitrator may be required to give reasons for his decision. The expert does not have to give reasons.

- A decision by an arbitrator may be the subject of an appeal to the High Court on a point of law under the Arbitration Acts. The decision of an expert is absolutely binding on all questions of fact and law unless clearly outside his terms of reference.

- The arbitrator is probably immune from claims for damages for negligence in the conduct of the reference and his decision. The expert may be liable in damages for professional negligence in carrying out his duties.

Each of these formal procedures can involve landlord and tenant in considerable costs, legal costs and professional fees and expenses. In most cases, the costs can be very significant indeed and if either landlord or tenant is considering evoking the dispute clause, one that involves arbitrators or experts, an attempt should be made to ascertain costs before proceeding.

Informal dispute procedures can be a lot more economical although costs will also arise. These are procedures put into train by landlord and tenant which consist of the appointment of an independent person who will attempt to mediate between the two parties in question in order to reach a compromise. The person appointed should be knowledgeable in the area of the dispute, for example rent review and there must be agreement to accept the decision of this person.

****

Main points from chapter 10

- Often, disputes will arise over one or more aspects of the lease, in particular rent and repairs.
- Before going to court, it is usually necessary to resolve disputes using either arbitration or an independent expert.
- Both arbitrators and independent experts are bound by different sets of rules. However, they both share a common tendency, that is that they can be expensive.
- It is always better for landlord and tenant to utilize informal dispute procedures. These procedures also have a cost but the time and effort is always less and thus cheaper.

11

Business Rates

One of the costs associated with taking on a business lease, which is quite often a significant cost, is that of business rates.

As with Council Tax applicable to residential properties, all commercial premises will be liable for business rates, which will be paid by the tenant, either direct or through a service charge.

Prospective business tenants should always determine the level of business rates applicable to a premises before entering into a lease. This cost is part of the overall cash flow plan, which will need to be formulated in the first stages of entering into a lease.

Tenants should always be aware of so called advisors who promise significant reductions in return for an advance payment. Often, the chance of a reduction will be based on following a procedure, which may or may not achieve a reduction. This procedure can be followed by a tenant without the use of an advisor.

Advice should always be sought from the local authority if it is thought that a business rate is too high. In addition, property professionals are in a position to advise a tenant about business rates. The Royal Institute of Chartered Surveyors provides a free rating help line service and advice is also available from the ISVA and the Institute of Revenues Rating and Valuation (IRRV). See useful addresses.

****

12

Security of Tenure for Business Tenants

The Landlord and Tenant Act 1954 part II

The Landlord and Tenant Act 1954, part II, contains a significant framework of legislation designed to protect tenants of shops, offices, factories, public houses and other business premises. The Act applies in England and Wales but not Scotland.

The Act sets out special rules for both landlord and tenant. The landlord cannot simply evict a tenant following the end of the term of a lease but must follow a strict notice procedure, demonstrating reasonable grounds and the tenant can also follow a strict notice procedure claiming the right to a new tenancy.

When an existing tenancy comes to an end it will continue as a statutory tenancy until the procedures contained within the 1954 Act are exhausted.

Certain notices to be given under the Act by landlords and tenants must be in special form. Each notice has a form number which can be obtained from a legal stationers. The notices are prescribed by the Landlord and Tenant Act 1954, Part 2. New notices have been produced as a result of the introduction of the Regulatory reform (Business Tenancies) (England and Wales) Order 2003, which has introduced simpler regulations designed to assist and protect both landlord and tenant in the process of ending a tenancy.

Copies of the notices, and a list of forms can be obtained online by downloading them from www.odpm.gov.uk/business tenancies (Office of the Deputy Prime Minister). This site has a complete breakdown of all procedures to be adopted when terminating tenancies. Other useful general advice is also available.

The following are facts to be considered when deciding if the procedures prescribed in the Landlord and Tenant Act 1954, part II, apply:

Part II normally applies to any tenant or sub- tenant occupying business premises. A tenant is not covered if he or she has sub-let the whole of the premises and do not occupy them themselves. However, personal occupation by the tenant is not essential, occupation by an agent or manager will suffice.

It will make a difference if the tenancy agreement is in the tenants name but the tenant trades from the premises as a company. In these circumstances the tenant could lose the right to renew the tenancy. A solicitor should be consulted in this case.

Part II of the Act applies to only a number of types of tenancy. The tenant, who may be an individual or company, may have a lease, or a written or oral tenancy agreement.

Certain categories of tenancy are excluded from the Act

- The tenant of an agricultural holding under a farm business tenancy

- The tenant under a mining lease

- Certain service tenants who were granted their tenancies only because they were employed by their landlord

- A tenant whose tenancy is for a fixed term of six months or less, with no right to renew or extend the tenancy

- Certain tenants who, without the landlords consent, are using the premises for business purposes although prohibited from doing so by the terms of the tenancy

- Tenants holding long leases at low rents which have been extended under the Leasehold Reform Act 1967, and in some cases, sub-tenants of such tenants

- A tenant whose tenancy was granted on the specific understanding that the protection of the Act would not apply, provided that this arrangement was sanctioned in advance by the court.

Licenses are not covered by part II of the Act. Legal advice needs to be taken in this case.

Agreements excluding security of tenure

It is possible at the outset for landlord and tenant to agree to contract out of the security of tenure provisions under the 1954 Act. Whereas previously it was necessary to apply to court for approval of an agreement this is no longer the case. However, if an agreement is to be valid it is vital that the parties to the agreement comply fully with either one of two new procedures: the advance notice procedure or the statutory declaration procedure.

The advance notice procedure

The landlord must serve on the tenant a prescribed warning notice at least 14 days before the tenant signs the lease or becomes contractually committed to a lease. Once the 14 days are up the parties are free to sign a lease containing an agreement to exclude security of tenure.

The statutory declaration procedure

It is normally preferable to use the advance notice procedure. This gives the tenant sufficient time to consider whether the exclusion is in their best interests. However, where both parties do not want to wait for the elapse of 14 days they can make a statutory declaration before an independent solicitor. This is suitable where the tenant wants to occupy the premises quickly.

Details of these procedures and the relevant forms are set out in Schedules 1 and 2 to the Regulatory reform (Business tenancies) (England and Wales) Order 2003. As above these notices can be accessed on the website of the Office of Deputy Prime Minister.

The landlord can seek information from the tenant about his or her tenancies or sub tenancies as the lease or tenancy draws to an end. This cannot be sought before there is less than two years of the term left. This has to be done by special notice (see appendix).

The Procedures for terminating and renewing tenancies

By s 24(1) of the Landlord and Tenant Act 1954 Part II, a tenancy to which the Act applies will not come to an end unless terminated in accordance with Part II of the Act. This is the principle of *statutory continuation* of a business tenancy, whether fixed term or periodic. The majority of business leases are covered by the Act.

There are three methods of termination of a business tenancy, to which s 24 will not apply. They are where the tenant gives a notice to quit, in the case of a periodic tenancy, the second is surrender and the third forfeiture. Apart from these methods Part II will apply.

Where the parties agree in writing on a new tenancy, which has the effect of terminating the current tenancy the current tenancy will continue until the commencement date of the new tenancy but Part II will not apply.

Part II of the Act provides for various statutory methods of terminating a continuing tenancy by means of statutory notices, as follows:

- The tenant has the right to terminate a fixed term tenancy, on it coming to an end, prior to the start of continuation under Part II, by notice under s 27
- The landlord has the right to terminate a fixed term or periodic tenancy by notice in the prescribed form under s 25
- The tenant may request a new tenancy under s 26 by a notice in the prescribed form, where the current tenancy is a fixed term tenancy exceeding one year, continued by s 24(1) or not. In the case of fixed terms for less than one year and periodic tenancies, the tenant cannot request a new tenancy under s 26 unless he is given a landlords s 25 notice.

Termination of a fixed term tenancy by the tenant under s 27
A tenancy for a fixed term will be continued beyond its contractual term date automatically under s 24 of the Landlord and Tenant Act 1954 Part II, unless steps are taken to prevent it by the tenant under s 27(1) or by the landlord under s 25. A tenant is required to give the landlord not less than three months notice that he does not want it to continue. Alternatively, a tenant can terminate a tenancy that is continuing after time, under s 27(2) by giving not less than three months notice in writing expiring on any quarter day.

No special form of notice is required but in neither case can the notice validly be given by the tenant until he has been in occupation for more than one month. Once notice is validly given the tenant will lose any rights under the act and the tenancy will terminate on the date specified.

Termination of the tenancy by the landlord under s 25

A landlord's only way to terminate a tenancy to which Part II applies, other than by granting a new tenancy or forfeiture, is by giving the tenant a notice to terminate under s 25 of Part II of the Act. This applies to all periodic tenancies and tenancies for a fixed term exceeding six months whether or not they are continuing under s 24 (1). The landlord's notice must comply strictly with the provisions of the Act. These are as follows:

- *Form.* The notice must be in writing, in the prescribed form or in a substantially similar form. All particulars must be correct.
- *Date of termination.* The notice must specify the date on which the current tenancy is to come to an end. The date specified must not be earlier than the date on which, in the case of a fixed term tenancy, it would have expired by effluxion of time. In the case of a periodic tenancy it must not be earlier than the earliest date on which the current tenancy could have been brought to an end by a notice to quit served by the landlord.
- *Giving a s 25 notice.* A s 25 notice may be given by the landlord not less than six, nor more than 12 months before the termination date specified in the notice. The notice must be served by the landlord. A landlord may terminate at one and the same time the tenancy and any sub tenancies derived out of it.

A tenants counter notice

The landlord's notice must require the tenant to notify the landlord in writing whether or not, at the date of termination specified in the landlords notice, he will be willing to give up possession. This provides in effect, for the serving of a counter notice by the tenant. The notice need not be in any special form. The 2003 Regulations have removed the time frame for the counter notice as a lot of tenants were falling foul of this.

The landlords notice must, under s 25(6) of the Act state whether or not the landlord would oppose the application to the court by the tenant for a new tenancy and if so, on what grounds he will rely. The grounds on which a landlord can oppose an application for a new tenancy are as follows:

- That the tenant ought not to have a new tenancy because he has not sufficiently complied with the terms of his current tenancy or has otherwise failed to behave properly as a tenant (paragraphs (a) to (c))

- That the landlord can provide suitable alternative accommodation for the tenant. Paragraph (d)

- That the application for a new tenancy is made by a sub-tenant occupying part of the premises, that the landlord is in a position to let or sell the premises as a whole, and that he ought to get possession of the part occupied by the sub tenant since otherwise he will suffer substantial loss. Paragraph (e)

- That the landlord requires possession in order to demolish or reconstruct the premises. Paragraph (f)

- That the landlord intends to occupy the premises himself for business purposes or as his residence. The landlord cannot use this ground if he bought the premises over the head of the sitting tenant less than five years before the end of the tenancy. Paragraph (g)

The grounds are laid out in full a little further on. The landlord who relies on suitable alternative accommodation may fail to satisfy the court that the alternative accommodation will be immediately available at the end of the current tenancy. But if he shows that it will be available up to 12 months later, the court will not grant a new tenancy and may within the 14 days time limit under the act, if the tenant requires, extend the current tenancy until the later date. The same happens if the landlord relies on paragraphs (e) or (f) and can show that he needs possession up to 12 months later than the end of the current tenancy.

A landlord who relies on paragraph (f) will not succeed if:

- The tenant agrees to a new tenancy giving the landlord access enabling him/her to carry out the intended work, which would not substantially interfere with the tenant's work.

OR

- The tenant agrees to accept a new tenancy of an economically separate part of the premises and either:

- This new tenancy gives the landlord access to enable him to carry out the intended work which would not substantially interfere with the tenants business with respect to that part or

- Possession of the remainder of the premises by the landlord would be reasonably sufficient to enable the landlord to carry out the intended work.

Application to the court

The tenant must apply not earlier than two months but not later than four months after requesting a new tenancy, or after the notice of termination is given to him. If he/she does not apply within this period he/she will lose the rights to do so and to stay in the premises. Unless a tenant has been able to reach a binding agreement with the landlord in writing on all the terms of a new tenancy before the end of the two to four month period the tenant will always have to apply to the court to protect his/her position.

Provided that the tenant observes the time limits for applying, the court *must* order a new tenancy to be granted unless the landlord can prove a ground summarized previously and outlined in full below.

If the landlord can satisfy the court that he is entitled to possession of the property on one or more grounds then the court *must* grant him possession. If the landlord cannot do so then the court *must* order the grant of a new tenancy.

The application for a new tenancy will be to the local county court, although the High Court can deal with more complex issues. The terms of the new tenancy can be those agreed in writing between the landlord and tenant or can be determined by the court, with regard to the current tenancy.

If the grant of a new tenancy is refused, compensation is payable on the tenant quitting the premises, but only if:

- The landlord has opposed or the court has refused the grant of a new tenancy solely on the grounds set out in paragraph (e) (f) or (g) as shown below
- There is no agreement, which effectively excludes compensation.

Landlord's grounds for opposing an application for a new tenancy

As we have seen, if the tenant applies to the court for a new tenancy, the landlord can only oppose the application on one or more grounds set out in

s 30(1) of the 1954 Act. Although mentioned briefly above, the grounds are fully outlined below.

The paragraph letters are those used in the Act. The landlord can only use a ground if the paragraph letter is shown in paragraph 5 of the notice given in the special form.

The Grounds are as follows

a) where under the current tenancy the tenant has any obligations with respect to the repair and maintenance of the holding, that the tenant ought not to be granted a new tenancy in view of the state of the holding, being a state resulting from the tenants failure to comply with the said obligations;

b) that the tenant ought not to be granted a new tenancy in view of his persistent delay in paying rent and other charges

c) that the tenant ought not to be granted a new tenancy in view of other substantial breaches by him of his other obligations under the current tenancy or for any other reason connected with the tenants use or management of his holding;

d) that the landlord has offered or is willing to provide or secure the provision of suitable alternative accommodation for the tenant, that the terms on which the alternative accommodation is available are reasonable having regards to the terms of the current tenancy and to all other relevant circumstances, and that the accommodation and the time at which it will be available are suitable for the tenants requirements (including the requirement to preserve goodwill) having regard to the nature and class of his business and to the situation and extent of, and facilities afforded by, the holding;

e) where the current tenancy was created by the subletting of part only of the property comprised in a superior tenancy and the landlord is the owner of an interest in reversion expectant on the termination of that superior tenancy, that the aggregate of the rents reasonably obtainable on separate lettings of the holding, and the remainder of that property would be substantially less than the rent reasonably obtainable on a letting of that property as a whole, that on the termination of the current tenancy the landlord requires possession of the holding for the purposes of letting or otherwise disposing of the said property as a whole, and that in view thereof the tenant ought not to be granted a new tenancy;

f) that on the termination of the current tenancy the landlord intends to demolish or reconstruct the premises comprised in the holding or a substantial part of those premises or to carry out substantial work of construction on the holding or part thereof and that he could not reasonably do so without obtaining possession of the holding;

(If the landlord uses this ground, the court can still sometimes grant a new tenancy if certain conditions set out in s 31(A) of the Act can be met)

g) that on the termination of the current tenancy the landlord intends to occupy the holding for the purposes, or partly for the purposes, of a business to be carried out by him herein, or as his residence. The landlord must normally have been the landlord for more than five years to use this ground.

The amount of compensation the tenant receives depends on how long the tenant has been in occupation carrying on a business in the premises. If it has been less than 14 years the tenant receives a sum equal to the appropriate multiplier (see below) times the ratable value of the property occupied at the end of the tenancy.

For 14 years or more the tenant will receive the appropriate multiplier time twice the ratable value of the property occupied at the end of the tenancy.

Since 1st April 1990 the appropriate multiplier has been prescribed by the Landlord and Tenant Act 1954 (Appropriate Multiplier) Order 1990 (S1 1990 no 363). This order prescribes a multiplier of:

1. Where the date for determining the rateable value is on or after 1st April 1990 (If part of the property is domestic this will be disregarded in determining the ratable value. If the tenant occupies on the date a section 25 or s 26 (6) notice under the 1954 Landlord and tenant Act is served, the whole or any part of the domestic property, he will also be entitled to a sum equal to his reasonable expenses in removing from the domestic property.

2. If the landlords notice was served before 1st April 1990, and so the date for determining the ratable value is before that date, but the tenant quits on or after 1st April 1990.

For some tenancies existing or contracted for, before 1st April 1990 where the tenant has opted for compensation to be based on the ratable value of the holding on 31st March 1990 during a transitional period (i.e. where the landlords s 25 notice is given after the 31st March 1990 but before 1st April 2000) as set out in schedule seven to the Local Government and Housing Act 1989. The tenant must opt not less than two nor more than four months after the landlords notice or after he has requested a new tenancy.

Professional advice may be needed on which of the three multipliers is the appropriate one in individual cases and, for example, concerning any queries about the ratable value.

A tenant may also be entitled to compensation under other Acts. If in doubt seek professional advice.

It is extremely important that all business tenants/lessees are aware of their rights when nearing the end of their tenancy/lease term. In all likelihood, it will probably be necessary to obtain legal advice if tenants/lessees intend to renew a tenancy, or make an application to a court for renewal and the landlord intends to oppose on the grounds laid out above. This should be sought as soon as possible.

In many cases, if a tenant has a good track record and a business is successful then the granting of a new lease/tenancy is a formality. However, for a number of reasons, the landlord may wish to get back his premises. Approaches to the landlord should be made well in advance in order to determine the situation regarding the granting of a tenancy.

****

Main points from chapter 12

- The Landlord and Tenant Act 1954 Part II is the key Act governing security of tenure for business tenants. No business tenancy governed by the Act can be brought to an end unless a strict notice procedure is complied with. This notice procedure was amended by the Regulatory reform (Business Tenancies) (England and Wales) Order 2003. The Regulations were introduced to streamline the procedures in the 1954 Act.
- Section 24 (1) of the Act enables statutory continuation of a business tenancy
- A tenant has the right to terminate a fixed term tenancy, prior to continuation, by notice under section 27.
- The landlord has the right to terminate a fixed term or periodic tenancy by notice, in prescribed form, under section 25.
- A tenant may serve a counter notice and request a new tenancy under section 26 of the Act.
- A landlord can oppose the grant of a new tenancy on a number of grounds outlined in the Act.
- A tenant may be liable for compensation if the grant of a new tenancy is refused. The level of compensation will depend on the length of time on the premises and the nature of the business.

Useful Addresses, Contacts and Publications.

Property advice

The Royal Institute of Chartered Surveyors (RICS) Information Centre on 0870 333 1600 www.rics.org.uk.

The Incorporated Society of Valuers and Auctioneers (ISVA) on 0207 235 2282

The RICS also supply, free of charge "Rent Review – a guide for small businesses" send a large stamped, self addressed envelope to Corporate Communications, The Royal Institute of Chartered Surveyors, RICS Contact Centre, Surveyor Court, Westwood way, Coventry CV4 8JE.

The Property Managers Association, through Boots the Chemist also provides a guide to good practice on service charges in commercial property. Send a stamped addressed envelope to: The Property Managers Association, Boots the Chemists Ltd, The Estates Department, Hargreaves House, Wollaton Street, Nottingham NG1 5FG.

The RICS publish a code of practice for commercial property leases in England and Wales, obtainable from the address above..

For information on local solicitors who could represent you, call the Law Society on 0207 242 1222. www.lawsociety.org.uk.

For information on local licensed conveyancers who could represent you, call the Council for Licensed Conveyancers on 01245 349599.

Property owners association

The trade association which looks after the interests of property owners is:

The British Property Federation, 1 Warwick Row, London SW1E 5ER 020 7828 0111.

Useful Addresses

British Council for Offices

38 Lombard Street

London EC3V 9BS. www.bco.org.uk

Tel: 020 7283 4588

British Retail Consortium

Second Floor 21 Dartmouth Street

London SW1H 9BP

Tel: 020 7854 8900

Federation of Small Businesses

Sir Frank Whittle Way

Blackpool Business Park

Blackpool

Lancs
FY4 2FE www.fsb.org.uk

Tel: 01253 336 000

The Alliance of Independent Retailers and Businesses
Bank Chambers
5-9 St Nicholas Street
Worcester
WR1 UE

Tel: 01905 612733

Index

Appendix 1

Forms and their purposes under the Landlord and Tenant Act 1954 Part 2

Form number	Purpose
1	Ending a tenancy, where the landlord is **not opposed** to the grant of a new one
2	Ending a tenancy, where the landlord **is opposed** to the grant of a new one
3	Tenants request for a new tenancy of a premises
4	Landlords request for information from the tenant
5	Tenants request for information from the landlord or the landlords mortgage lender
6	Withdrawal of notice given under s 25 of the act ending a tenancy
7	Ending a tenancy, where the landlord **is opposed** to the grant of a new tenancy but where the tenant may be entitled under the 1967 Act to buy the freehold or extend the lease
8	Ending a tenancy, where a certificate given under section 57 of the act that the use or occupation or part of it is to be changed by a specified date
9	Ending a tenancy where a certificate given under section 57 of the Act that the use or occupation of the property or part of it is to be changed at a future date and the landlord **opposes** granting a new tenancy
10	Ending a tenancy to which Part 2 of the act applies, where a certificate given under section 57 of the act that the use or occupation of the property is to be changed at a future date and the landlord **does not oppose** granting a new tenancy
11	Ending a tenancy, where a certificate given under

	section 58 of the Act that for reasons of national security it is necessary that the use or occupation of the property should be discontinued or changed
12	Ending a tenancy, where a certificate given under section 60 of the Act that it is necessary or expedient for regeneration purposes that the use or occupation of the property should be changed.

Appendix 2
Sample business lease – mixed commercial/rented premises (shop with flat above)

PARTICULARS

Date of Lease		
The Parties	1. The Landlord	
	2. The Tenant	
The Premises	Shown edged red on the attached plan	
The Rent	The yearly rent of £6,000.00 or such higher sum as may be payable under clause 6 of this lease	
The Term	12 years from 2009	
The Permitted Use	1. As to the ground floor shop use as a shop within Class A1in the Schedule to the Town and Country Planning (Use Classes) Order 1 987 for the trade or business of the sale of fishing tackle and ancillary merchandise or for such other trade or business not prohibited by this lease as shall be approved by the Landlord in writing (such approval not to be unreasonably withheld) 2. As to the first and second floor maisonette use as a private residence in	

	the occupation of a single family
The Review Dates	2009 2015 and the day before the expiry of the period referred to in the above definition of "the Term"

THIS LEASE is made between the Parties referred to in the foregoing particulars

1. IN this lease unless the context otherwise requires:-

(1) The expression "the Particulars" shall mean the foregoing particulars

(2) The expressions contained in the Particulars shall have the respective meanings assigned to them in the Particulars

(3) The expression "the Landlord" shall include the person persons or corporation for the time being entitled to the reversion immediately expectant on the termination of the Term

(4) The expression "the Tenant" shall include the successors in title of the Tenant

(5) The expression "the Term" shall include the period of any holding over or extension continuance or renewal thereof whether by statute common law or agreement

(6) The expression "the Insured Risks" shall mean the risks of fire explosion lightning impact flood storm or tempest riot or civil commotion bursting or overflowing of water tanks apparatus or pipes

boilers heating plant and equipment or such of them and any other risks against which the Landlord may reasonably consider it necessary or desirable and be able to insure

(7) The expression "the Granted Rights" shall mean the right for the Tenant in common with all other persons having the like right from time to time and at all times to pass and repass over and along the passageway shown hatched blue on the attached plan and the right of passage and running of water and soil from the Premises through the sewers or drains running under the said passageway and to enter upon such passageway for the purpose of repairing cleansing and maintaining such sewers or drains the Tenant making good all damage occasioned thereby

(8) The expression "the Reserved Rights" shall mean:-

(a) The right to use any pipes wires drains sewers gutters cables ducts and other conducting media plant equipment and installations supplying any adjoining premises belonging to the Landlord with services and passing through under or over or being in the Premises and the right to enter the Premises for the purpose of maintaining and repairing such pipes wires drains sewers gutters cables ducts and other conducting media the person exercising such right causing as little damage or disturbance as possible and making good all damage actually caused to the Premises as the result or in the course of any such entry

(b) The right to enter upon the Premises for the purposes (or any of them) referred to and in accordance with the provisions of this lease

(9) The expression "the Planning Acts" shall mean the Town and Country Planning Act 1990 The Planning (Listed Buildings and Conservation Areas) Act 1990 The Planning (Hazardous Substances) Act 1990 the Planning (Consequential Provisions) Act 1990 as from time to time modified or re-enacted and any regulations or orders made under the authority of any such Act

(10) The expression "Enactment" shall mean an Act of Parliament statutory instrument order or byelaw for the time being in force and shall include any rule regulation scheme plan or direction issued under or deriving authority from any such act instrument order or byelaw and a reference to a particular Enactment shall be deemed to refer to that Enactment as from time to time modified re-enacted or replaced

(11) The singular shall include the plural the masculine shall include the feminine and the neuter and covenants entered into and burdens assumed by a party consisting of more than one person shall be deemed to be entered into and assumed jointly and severally so as to apply to and be enforceable against all both or any of such persons and their and each of their personal representatives

2. THE Landlord demises to the Tenant the Premises and the Landlord's fixtures and fittings in the Premises TOGETHER with the Granted Rights but EXCEPT AND RESERVING to the Landlord and the tenant or tenants for the time being of any adjoining premises belonging to the Landlord the Reserved Rights for the Term YIELDING AND PAYING

(1) The Rent which shall be paid by equal quarterly installments in advance on the usual quarter days the first of such installments being calculated proportionately from the.............................199 to the next following quarter day having already been paid such payments to be made so long as the Landlord shall not otherwise require by bankers standing order

(2) By way of further rent on demand 'all sums payable by the Tenant to the Landlord under the provisions of this lease

3. THE Tenant covenants with the Landlord throughout the Term:-

(1)To pay the Rent without any deduction or abatement whatsoever except only such sums as are by law payable by the Landlord to the exclusion of the Tenant notwithstanding any stipulation to the contrary

(2)To pay to the Landlord from time to time on demand

(a)A sum or sums equal to such amount or amounts as shall from time to time be expended by the Landlord in insuring the Premises and the Landlord's fixtures and fittings therein of an insurable nature against the Insured Risks and all boilers and heating apparatus therein and plant used in connection with such boilers against the risk of explosion and in effecting or maintaining insurance in such sum or sums as the Landlord shall think fit indemnifying the Landlord against third party and property owner's risks in respect of the Premises and any liability which the Landlord may incur by reason of the condition of the Premises whether under the Defective Premises Act 1 972 or otherwise or (if any such sum or sums shall relate to the insurance of other premises as well as the Premises) the proportion of such sum or sums attributable to the Premises such proportion to be fixed by the Landlord or his surveyor or agent whose decision shall be final

(b) Such sum as shall from time to time be expended by the Landlord i insuring or causing to be insured the Premises against loss of the Rent for a period of three years taking into account any potential increase in the Rent under the provisions of this lease

(3) To pay or repay to the Landlord and discharge all rates taxes duties charges assessments impositions and outgoings whether parliamentary parochial local or of any other description save for any tax payable on or as a result of any disposal of or dealing with the Landlord and all charges for gas electricity telephone water sewage and other services which are now or may at any time hereafter be taxed charged or imposed upon or payable in respect of the Premises or on the owner or occupier of

the Premises and not to leave the Premises or permit the Premises to be left unused or unoccupied nor to claim or permit to be claimed void rating relief in respect of the Premises if as a result the Landlord will be deprived from claiming such relief for any period after the determination of the Term

(4) (a) To put maintain and keep the whole of the Premises and all additions and improvements and the Landlord's fixtures and fittings in the Premises and all appurtenances forming part of the Premises in good and tenantable repair and decorative order in every respect (damage by any of the Insured Risks only excepted save to the extent to which the payment of a claim by the Landlord is refused by the insurers in whole or in part as the result of any act neglect or default of the Tenant or any sub-tenant or any licensee servant or agent of the Tenant or any sub-tenant) PROVIDED that the Tenant shall not be required to put maintain or keep the Premises in a better state of repair than the state at the date of this lease as evidenced by the attached schedule of condition

(b) When and so often as any Landlord's fixtures shall reasonably require replacement to substitute other fixtures of a similar description quality and value to the reasonable satisfaction of the Landlord

(c) To keep all external parts (if any) of the Premises clean and tidy and all landscaped areas (if any) forming part of the Premises in a proper state of cultivation and to replace any trees shrubs or plants therein which may die or become affected by disease

(5) Whenever required by the Landlord to pay or contribute a fair proportion attributable to the Premises of the cost and expense of repairing maintaining renewing rebuilding lighting and cleansing any yards passages forecourts pipes wires drains sewers gutters cables ducts and other conducting media plant equipment and installations fences roofs walls or other appurtenances or conveniences which shall belong to or be used by or for the Premises, in common with other nearby or adjoining premises (such proper proportion to be certified by the Landlord's surveyors)

(6) In every third year computed from the commencement of

the Term and also in the last six months of the Term (whether determined by effluxion of time or otherwise) provided that in such circumstances there shall not be an obligation arising twice in 1 2 months to prepare and paint with three coats of paint of good quality or otherwise treat as the case may require all external parts of the Premises which have previously been or usually are or ought to be or require to be painted or otherwise treated respectively in tints or colours to be approved in writing by the Landlord such approval not to be unreasonably withheld or delayed and also as often as in the Landlord's opinion shall be necessary to clean wash down point make good and restore the exterior stone or brick work and other finishes of the exterior of the Premises and restore the same to their former condition and appearance to the reasonable satisfaction of the Landlord and in every fifth year computed from the commencement of the Term and also in the last six months of the Term (whether determined by effluxion of time or otherwise) provided that in such circumstances there shall not be an obligation arising twice in 1 2 months to prepare and paint with two coats of paint of good quality redecorate or paper with paper of good quality or otherwise treat as the case may be all internal parts of the Premises which have previously been or usually are or ought to be so painted decorated papered or treated (the tints colours and patterns in respect of the work done in the last six months of the Term to be approved in writing by the Landlord) such consent not to be unreasonably withheld or delayed and to wash down all tiles glazed bricks and similar washable surfaces all such works to be carried out in a good and workmanlike manner

(7) Not to do or permit to be done any act or thing which may obstruct or damage the drainage system of the Premises or any part thereof nor to deposit or permit the escape of trade effluent or other obnoxious or deleterious materials into such drainage system

(8) At the expiration or sooner determination of the Term peaceably and quietly to yield up the Premises and the Landlord's fixtures and fittings in the Premises together with all additions and improvements to the Landlord in such state and condition as shall in all

respects be consistent with due performance by the Tenant of the covenants contained in this lease and if so required by the Landlord to remove all or any trade or tenant's fixtures removable by the Tenant and all partitioning or other alterations installed or effected by the Tenant with or without the Landlord's approval and to make good to the Landlord's reasonable satisfaction all damage to the Premises caused or revealed by such removal

(9) To observe and comply in all respects with all and any provisions requirements and directions of or under any Enactment so far as they or it shall relate to or affect the Premises or any fixture machinery plant or chattel for the time being in the Premises or the use of the Premises for the purpose of any trade or business or the employment in the Premises of any person or persons or the supply to the Premises of any service and to execute all works which by or under any Enactment or by any government department local authority factory inspector statutory undertaker or other public authority or duly authorized officer or court of competent jurisdiction acting under or in pursuance of any Enactment are or may be directed or required to be executed whether by the Landlord or by the Tenant at any time during the Term upon or in respect of the Premises or any such fixture machinery plant or chattel or in respect of any such use employment or supply and to indemnify the Landlord at all times against all costs charges and expenses of or incidental to the execution of any such works and not at any time during the Term to do or omit or suffer to be done or omitted on or about the Premises any act or thing in breach of the terms of this lease by reason of which the Landlord may under any Enactment incur or have imposed upon him or become liable to pay any penalty damages compensation costs charges or expenses

(10) To give full particulars to the Landlord of any permission notice order direction or proposal for a notice order or direction made given or issued to the Tenant by any government department local or public authority under or by virtue of any Enactment within 14 days of the receipt by the Tenant of notice of the same and if so required by the Landlord to produce such permission notice order or

direction or proposal for a notice order or direction to the Landlord AND ALSO without delay to take all reasonable or necessary steps to comply with any such notice order or direction and also at the request of the Landlord to make or join with the Landlord in making such objections or representations against or in respect of any such notice order proposal or direction as the Landlord shall deem expedient

(11) To notify the Landlord forthwith in writing of any defect in or want of repair for which the Landlord may be responsible to third parties under the Defective Premises Act 1 972 or any other Enactment and to indemnify the Landlord against all liability and expense which may be sustained or incurred by the Landlord in respect of any notice claim or demand costs and proceedings made or brought under such Act or other Enactment Or as a result of any failure by the Tenant to give any such notification

(12) In relation to the Planning Acts:-

(a) To comply in all respects with the provisions and requirements of the Planning Acts relating to the Premises and the use of the Premises and all licences consents permissions and conditions granted to the Tenant or imposed on the Tenant or the Premises under the Planning Acts relating to or affecting the Premises or any part of the Premises or any operations works acts or things already or to be carried out executed done or omitted on the Premises or the use of the Premises for any purpose

(b) So often as occasion shall require at the expense in all respects of the Tenant to obtain from (as the case may be) the local planning authority or the appropriate government department all such licences consents and permissions as may be required from the carrying out by the Tenant of any operations on the Premises or the institution or continuance by the Tenant on the Premises of any use which may constitute development within the meaning of the Planning Acts

(c) To pay and satisfy any charge that may at any time be imposed under the Planning Acts in respect of the carrying out or maintenance by the

tenant on the Premises of any such operations or the institution or continuance by the Tenant of any such use

(d) Notwithstanding any consent which may be granted by the Landlord under this lease not to carry out or make any alteration or addition to or change of use of the Premises being an alteration or addition or change of use for which planning permission under the Planning Acts needs to be obtained or carry out any development (as defined by the Planning Acts) on or to the Premises without first obtaining such planning permission and not to apply for any such planning permission without first obtaining the Landlord's approval in writing which shall be deemed to lapse if such planning permission shall not be granted within six months of the date of the Landlord's approval

(e) Unless the Landlord shall otherwise direct to carry out before the expiration or sooner determination of the Term any works stipulated to be carried out to the Premises by a date subsequent to such expiration or sooner determination as a condition of any licence consent or permission which may have been granted during the Term

(f) To indemnify and keep indemnified the Landlord against any liability resulting from any contravention of the provisions of the Planning Acts

(13) To permit the Landlord and the owner or tenant of any adjoining premises and his or their surveyors or agents with or without workmen and others at all reasonable hours during the daytime on reasonable written notice being given (except in emergency) to enter (and in emergency to break and enter) the Premises or any part of the Premises for the purposes of inspecting and executing repairs or alterations to such adjoining premises or the pipes wires drains sewers gutters cables ducts

and other conducting media plant equipment and installations in the Premises supplying such adjoining premises with services and for such purpose to erect and maintain scaffolding and machinery and deposit materials on any suitable part of the Premises the person so entering the Premises causing as little damage or disturbance as possible and making good in a reasonable manner all damage actually caused to the Premises in the course or as a result of any such entry

(14) To permit the Landlord and his surveyor or agent with or without workmen and others at all reasonable hours during the daytime on reasonable written notice being given (except in emergency) to enter the Premises or any part of the Premises to ensure that nothing has been done in the Premises that constitutes a breach of any of the Tenant's covenants contained in this lease or to view and examine the state and condition of the Premises or to take inventories of the fixtures and fittings in the Premises or to make any inspection for the purposes of the Landlord and Tenant Acts 1 927 and 1 954 or any other Enactment for the time being affecting the Premises or any review of the Rent or any renewal (whether statutory or otherwise) of this lease as often as occasion shall require the person so entering the Premises causing as little damage and disturbance as possible and making good in a reasonable manner any damage actually caused to the Premises in the course or as a result of any such entry

(15) To permit any independent surveyor or arbitrator who may be appointed for the purpose of any review of the Rent under the provisions contained in this lease to enter the Premises in order to inspect the same and to supply to him such information as he shall properly require

(16) To repair and make good all breaches of covenant defects and wants of repair or decoration for which the Tenant may be liable under the covenants contained in this lease of which notice shall have been given by the Landlord to the Tenant within two calendar months after the giving of such notice or sooner if requisite AND if the

Tenant shall at any time make default in the performance of this covenant it shall be lawful for (but not obligatory upon) the Landlord (but without prejudice to his right of re-entry or any other right or remedy available to the Landlord under this lease or otherwise) to enter upon the Premises and to carry out and execute such works as may be required to repair and redecorate the Premises in accordance with such covenants and to repay to the Landlord forthwith on demand all expenses (including any legal costs surveyors fees and other similar expenses) incurred by the Landlord in respect of such works

(17) To permit the Landlord or his agents at any time (in the case of a proposed sale of the Landlord's interest in the Premises) or within six calendar months next before the expiration or sooner determination of the Term to enter upon the Premises and to fix and retain without interference upon any suitable part or parts of the Premises a notice board or notice boards for reletting or selling the Premises and not to remove or obscure such board or boards and on reasonable written notice to permit all persons by order in writing of the Landlord or his agents to view the Premises at all convenient hours in the daytime without interruption

(18) To pay to the Landlord all reasonable costs charges and expenses (including legal costs and fees payable to a surveyor or architect) which may be incurred or payable by the Landlord in or in contemplation of any steps taken to recover any arrears of the Rent or the enforcement of any of the covenants contained in this lease or the preparation and service of all notices and schedules relating to wants of repair to the Premises and agreeing such schedules with the Tenant whether before at or within 3 months after the termination of the Term or any proceedings relating to the Premises or the preparation and service of a notice under section 146 or 147 of the Law of Property Act 1 925 (whether or not any right of re-entry or forfeiture has been waived by the Landlord or the Tenant has been relieved under the provisions of such Act) or as a result or in contemplation of any application to any planning authority or of any application to the Landlord for any licence or consent

pursuant to the covenants contained in this lease or in respect of any improvement which the Tenant may be entitled to make on or to the Premises under or by virtue of the Landlord and Tenant Acts 1927 and 1 954 or any other Enactment for the time being affecting the Premises or in connection with the approval from time to time of any such works and to keep the Landlord fully and effectually indemnified against all liability which he may incur in respect of any such application licence consent or works

(19) Not to place bring keep or deposit on the Premises any article or substance in such position or in such quantity or weight as to exceed the load bearing capabilities of the ceilings roofs walls[1] floor members or structure of the Premises and not to do anything which may endanger the safety or stability of the Premises or any neighboring or adjoining premises

(20) Not to keep place or store or permit or suffer to be kept placed or stored in or upon or about the Premises any substance liquid or gas of a dangerous offensive combustible inflammable radioactive or explosive or corrosive nature or the keeping or storing of which may contravene any Enactment or require the licence or consent of any local or other competent authority or constitute a nuisance to the occupiers of neighboring or adjoining premises

(21) (a) Not to do or omit or suffer to be done or omitted any act matter or thing whatsoever the doing or omission of which would make void or voidable any policy of insurance of the Premises or any part thereof or any neighboring or adjoining premises or cause the premium payable in respect of any such insurance to be increased above the normal rate

(b) In the event of the Premises or any part of the Premises or any fixture or fitting in the Premises insured by the Landlord being destroyed or damaged by any of the Insured Risks to give immediate notice to the Landlord

(c) In the event of the Premises or any part of the Premises or any fixture or fitting in the Premises insured by the Landlord being destroyed or damaged by any of the Insured Risks and the insurance money under any policy of insurance effected by the Landlord being wholly or partly irrecoverable by reason of any act or default of the Tenant or any sub-tenant or any licensee servant or agent of the Tenant or any sub-tenant or by reason of any excess applied by the insurers forthwith to pay to the Landlord the whole or (as the case may require) the irrecoverable part of the cost of rebuilding reinstating or repairing the Premises. as the case may be or replacing or repairing such fixture or fitting

(22) To take all reasonable precautions against the outbreak of fire on the Premises and in particular to provide and keep in good repair and condition any fire alarms fire escapes and fire fighting or fire preventive equipment which shall be required to be kept in the Premises by any competent authority or by the Landlord

(23) Not at any time to make any alteration or addition to the electrical installation of the Premises save in accordance with the terms and conditions laid down by the Institution of Electrical Engineers and the regulations of the electricity supply authority

(24) (a) Not to make any structural alteration or addition whatsoever to or on the Premises

(b) Not without the previous consent in writing of the Landlord (such consent if granted to be without prejudice nevertheless to the provisions of sub-clause (12) of this clause) nor except in accordance with plans and specifications previously submitted to and approved by the Landlord's architects or surveyors to make any other addition or alteration to the Premises (including conducting media plant equipment and installations therein for the supply of services) such consent not to be unreasonably withheld

(25) Not to use or permit to be used the Premises

except for the Permitted Use and in particular not at any time to use the Premises or permit the Premises to be used for any illegal or immoral purpose or for any purpose which may infringe any legislation for the time being in force or for any noisy noxious dangerous or offensive trade business manufacture or occupation or for any public meeting exhibition or entertainment or for the manufacture consumption or sale of beer wine or spirituous liquors or as an hotel club billiards saloon dance hall sex shop funfair or amusement arcade or. for the purpose of any betting transaction within the meaning of the Betting Gaming and Lotteries Act 1 963 with or between persons resorting to the. Premises

(26) Not to do or permit or suffer to be done on the Premises or any part thereof anything which shall or may be or become or cause an annoyance nuisance damage inconvenience disturbance injury or danger to the Landlord or the owners lessees or occupiers of any other premises in the neighborhood or persons having business with them

(27) To take all necessary steps to prevent and not to permit any new window light opening doorway path passage drain or other encroachment right or easement to be made or acquired in to against over or upon the Premises and in case any such window light opening doorway path passage drain or other encroachment shall be made or threatened or attempted to be made or any such right or easement shall be acquired or attempted or threatened to be acquired then forthwith to give notice in writing thereof to the Landlord and to do at the request of the Landlord at the cost of the Landlord all such things as may be required for the purpose of preventing the making or continuance of such encroachment or the acquisition of such right or easement

(28) Not to sell goods by auction or permit or suffer any sale by auction to be held within or upon the Premises and not to store keep place exhibit or expose for sale or suffer to be stored kept placed exhibited or exposed for sale any plant machinery equipment materials

stores goods or articles whatsoever upon any pavement or forecourt in front of or upon any external part of the Premises

(29) Not to assign mortgage charge underlet or part with or share the possession of or permit the occupation by a licensee of part only of the Premises nor (save by way of a permitted assignment or underlease) to part with or share the possession of or permit the occupation by a licensee of the whole of the Premises

(30) Not to assign or underlet nor to permit any underlessee or sub-underlessee to assign or underlet the whole of the Premises save with the Landlord's previous consent in writing such consent not to be unreasonably withheld or granted subject to unreasonable conditions PROVIDED that such consent for an assignment of the Premises by the Tenant may:-

(a) Be withheld in the circumstances (specified for the purposes of s 1 9 (1 A) of the Landlord & Tenant Act 1927) set out in part 1 of the Schedule or any of them and/or

(b) Be granted subject to the conditions (specified for such purposes) set out in part 2 of the Schedule or any of them

(31) Not to underlet the whole of the Premises in consideration of a payment of a capital sum or premium

(32) Not to underlet the whole of the Premises save by way of an underlease:-

(a) At the best rent at which the Premises might reasonably be expected at the time to be let for the term granted by such underlease with vacant possession in the open market without payment of a premium (the amount of such rent to be previously approved in writing by the Landlord) such approval not to be unreasonably withheld and in any event at a rent not less than the Rent

(b) Containing provisions for the review of the rent reserved by such underlease in an upward direction only to a full market rental without taking a fine or a premium at the like times and in the like manner as the times and manner specified in this lease for the review of the Rent

(c) Containing (if the underlessee shall be a private limited company) a joint and several covenant on the part of at least two of its directors officers or members or other persons of satisfactory standing reasonably approved by the Landlord as principal debtors and so that they shall not be released even if the Tenant gives the company extra time to comply with any obligation or does not insist on its strict terms that:-

(i) the company will pay the Rent and observe and perform the covenants on the part of the underlessee contained in such underlease

(ii) they will indemnify the Tenant against any loss resulting from a default by the company and

(iii) if the underlease is disclaimed on the insolvency of the company they will if the Tenant so requires jointly take a new underlease of the Premises at their own expense on the same terms and conditions as the terms and condition of this underlease at the date of the disclaimer for a term equal to the remainder of the term thereby granted unexpired at such date

(d) Containing covenants identical to the covenants contained in sub-clauses (29) (30) {3 1) and (32) of this clause and a condition for re-entry on breach of covenant on the part of the underlessee and

(e) Otherwise in such form and containing such additional covenants and conditions and provisions as the Landlord shall reasonably and previously approve in writing

(33) On the grant of any permitted underlease or sub-underlease to obtain if the Landlord shall so require at the Tenant's expense an unqualified covenant in such document and form as the Landlord shall require on the part of the underlessee or sub-underlessee directly with the Landlord to observe and perform all the covenants on the part of the Tenant contained in this lease save for the covenants relating to the Rent and (if the intended underlessee or sub-underlessee shall be a private limited company) a joint and several covenant on the part of at least two of its directors officers or members or other persons of satisfactory standing approved by the Landlord directly with the Landlord as principal debtors and so that they shall not be released even if the Landlord gives the company extra time to comply with any obligation or does not insist on its strict terms that

(a) The company will observe and perform such covenant and

(b) They will indemnify the Landlord against any loss resulting from a default by the company

(34) To give or cause to be given notice in writing of every assignment mortgage charge assent transfer underlease sub-underlease assignment mortgage or charge of an underlease or sub-underlease or devolution of or relating to the Premises and to deliver or cause to be delivered a certified copy of such instrument or any probate or letters of administration in any way relating to the Premises within 28 days after its execution or grant to the Landlord's solicitors and to pay a registration fee of £20.00 or such higher fee as such solicitors may reasonably require

(35) Not without the Landlord's consent in writing such consent not to be unreasonably withheld to erect affix or exhibit or

permit to be erected affixed or exhibited to or on any part of the exterior of the Premises or in or upon the windows of the Premises any aerial advertisement sign fascia placard bill notice signboard poster or other notification whatsoever and on the expiration or sooner determination of the Term to remove or efface any such aerial advertisement sign fascia placard bill notice signboard poster or notification and to make good any damage caused by such removal or effacement to the reasonable satisfaction of the Landlord

(36) Not to form any permanent refuse dump or rubbish or scrap heap on the Premises or in or on any adjacent yard passageway or vacant land but to remove all refuse rubbish and scrap which may have accumulated on the Premises not less frequently than once a week

(37) To clean the windows in the Premises as often as occasion shall require and at least once in every calendar month

(38) To insure and keep insured any plate glass windows and doors in the Premises against damage or breakage to their full replacement value in the joint names of the Landlord and the Tenant with some reputable insurance office to be approved in writing from time to time by the Landlord (such approval not to be unreasonably withheld) and whenever so required to produce to the Landlord the policy and the receipt for the last premium payable for such insurance and in the case of damage to or destruction of such plate glass windows and doors to secure that all monies payable under or by virtue of the policy for such insurance shall be with all convenient speed laid out and applied in reinstating such plate glass windows and doors with glass of the same nature quality and thickness as at present and in case such monies shall be insufficient for such purpose to make good the deficiency

(39) Not to give any bill of sale or other preferential security on the goods and chattels of the Tenant which shall for the time being be in or about the Premises

(40) To produce to the Landlord from time to time such plans documents and other evidence as the Landlord may reasonably require in order to satisfy himself that the covenants on the part of the Tenant contained in this lease have been fully performed and observed

4. THE Landlord COVENANTS with the Tenant:-

(1) That the Tenant paying the Rent and observing and performing the covenants on his part contained in this lease shall and may quietly enjoy the Premises during the Term without any interruption by the Landlord or persons lawfully claiming under the Landlord

(2) (a) To insure the Premises and the Landlord's fixtures and fittings therein of an insurable nature in such sum as the Landlord shall in his absolute discretion consider to be the costs likely to be incurred in rebuilding or reinstating the Premises at the time when such rebuilding or reinstatement is likely to take place having regard to all relevant circumstances including expected increases in building costs against loss or damage caused by the Insured Risks including the cost of shoring up demolition and debris removal and architects' and other fees relating to the reinstatement of the Premises or such higher sum as the Tenant shall in writing require in an insurance office of repute

(b) From time to time at the request and cost of the Tenant to provide the Tenant with full details of such policy or policies of insurance effected by the Landlord and evidence of payment of the current premium or premiums

(c) In case of destruction or damage of or to the Premises or any such fixture or fitting by any of the Insured Risks (unless payment of any money payable under any policy for such insurance shall be refused either in whole or in part by reason of any act neglect or default of the Tenant or any sub-tenant or any servant agent or licensee of the Tenant or any sub-tenant) to secure that all monies payable under or by virtue of any such policy of insurance (other than money received in respect of loss of rent or professional fees as aforesaid) shall be with all convenient speed laid out and applied in rebuilding repairing replacing or otherwise reinstating the Premises or such fixture or fitting

5. PROVIDED ALWAYS AND IT IS HEREBY AGREED that:-

(1) If at any time during the Term any installment of the Rent shall not be paid within 21 days after becoming due (whether lawfully demanded or not) or if any covenant on the Tenant's part contained in this lease shall not be performed or observed or if the Tenant or any surety for the Tenant shall compound or arrange with his creditors or suffer any distress or execution to be levied on the Premises or the contents thereof or (being an individual) shall commit any act of bankruptcy or enter into a voluntary arrangement within the meaning of section 1 of the Insolvency Act 1 986 or (being a company) shall go into liquidation either compulsory or voluntary (except for a voluntary liquidation of a solvent company for the purpose of reconstruction or amalgamation) or if a receiver shall be appointed of its undertaking or an administration order is made under the Insolvency Act 1 986 or if the Premises shall be left vacant for a period of three months or more then and in any such case the Landlord or any person or persons duly authorised by the Landlord shall be entitled to re-enter into or upon the Premises or any part of the Premises in the name of the whole and to repossess and enjoy the Premises as if this lease had not been granted and thereupon the Term shall absolutely cease and determine without prejudice to any right of action or remedy of the Landlord in respect of any antecedent breach by the Tenant of any of the covenants contained in this lease

(2) In the event of the destruction of or damage to the Premises by any of the Insured Risks so as to render the Premises or any part of the Premises unfit for occupation and use by the Tenant **PROVIDED THAT** and to the extent that the policy or policies of insurance effected by the Landlord shall not have been vitiated or payment

of the policy monies refused in whole or in part as a result of any act neglect or default of the Tenant or any sub-tenant or any licensee servant or agent of the Tenant or any sub-tenant the Rent or a fair proportion of the Rent according to the nature and extent of the damage sustained shall be suspended until the Premises are rebuilt or reinstated fit for occupation and use or until the expiry of a period of three years from the date of the event causing such destruction or damage whichever shall be the earlier

(3) If at any time during the Term any installment of the Rent or any other money which may become payable by the Tenant (other than money payable under clause 6 (3) (b) of this lease and actually paid within 21 days of the date upon which it becomes due) to the Landlord under any of the provisions of this lease at any time or times shall not be paid on the due date (whether such rent or other money has been formally or legally demanded or not) or shall be tendered but declined by the Landlord so as not to waive a breach of covenant then the amount for the time being unpaid shall (without prejudice to the Landlord's right of re-entry or any other right or remedy of the Landlord) as from such date or (in the case of money payable under clause 6 (3) (b) of this lease) as from a day 21 days after such date until paid bear and carry interest and the Tenant accordingly COVENANTS with the Landlord that in such circumstances and during such period or periods the Tenant will pay to the Landlord interest (as well after as before any judgment) on any such unpaid amount at the rate of £4.00 per cent per annum above National Westminster Bank PLC base rate for the time being prevailing or £10.00 per cent per annum whichever shall be the higher

(4) All sums reserved or payable by the Tenant under this lease during the Term whether by way of reimbursement to the Landlord or otherwise shall be exclusive of value added tax and if value added tax or any other tax shall be or become payable on or in respect of any such sum such tax shall be paid or reimbursed by the Tenant in addition to the sum on or in respect of which such tax is payable

(5) If at the expiration or sooner determination of the Term any fixture machinery plant or chattel belonging to the Tenant shall be left in the Premises by the Tenant for more than seven days the

Landlord shall have power to sell the same as agent for and on behalf of the Tenant the money thereby arising (but not any interest thereon) less the costs of the sale and any money owing to the Landlord under any of the provisions of this lease or otherwise to be paid or accounted for by the Landlord to the Tenant on demand

(6) Subject to the provisions of section 38 (2) the Tenant shall not on quitting the Premises be entitled to any compensation under sections 37 and 59 of the Landlord and Tenant Act 1954

(7) Any notice under this lease shall be in writing and may be served on the person on whom it is to be served either personally or by leaving it for him at the Premises (if served upon the Tenant) or at his registered office (if a company) or last known place of business or abode or by sending it by registered post or the recorded delivery service to the Premises (if served upon the Tenant) or to such office or place and in the case of a notice to be served on the Landlord it may be served in like manner upon any agent for the Landlord duly authorized in that behalf PROVIDED ALWAYS that any notice addressed to "the Landlord" or "the Tenant" and served in accordance with the provisions of this sub-clause shall be deemed valid notwithstanding that it did not give the name of the Landlord or Tenant as the case may be

(8) If the Tenant shall desire to determine the Term on either of the Review Dates and of such desire shall give to the Landlord not less than 6 months previous notice in writing specifying the desired termination date and if on the date so specified the Rent shall have been paid and the covenants and conditions on the part of the Tenant contained in this lease shall have been substantially observed and performed then on the date so specified the Term shall be determined and his lease shall cease to have effect without prejudice to any outstanding claims by either party against the other in respect of any antecedent breach of covenant

6. (1) IN this clause

(a) The expression "the Relevant Review Date" shall

mean whichever one of the Review Dates may from time to time give rise to a review of the Rent under the provisions of this clause and the expression "the Relevant Review Period" shall mean the period from that date to the next of the Review Dates or (if the Relevant Review Date shall be the last of the Review Dates) to the end of the Term as the case may be

(b) The expression "the Market Rent" shall mean the best yearly rent at which the Premises might reasonably be expected on the Relevant Review Date to be let as a whole with vacant possession in the open market by a willing landlord to a willing tenant for the Permitted Use and without payment of a premium for a term of equal length to the then unexpired residue length of the Term commencing on the Relevant Review Date under a lease containing the same terms and conditions (other than the initial amount of the Rent but including provisions identical to the provisions of this clause for the review of the rent thereby reserved at intervals of the same frequency from the commencement of such term as the frequency of the Review Dates) in all other respects as are contained in this lease as from time to time varied extended or rectified on the assumption (if not a fact) that at the Relevant Review Date

(I) all the covenants on the part of the Tenant contained in this lease as to repair and otherwise have been fully observed and performed at that date and

(ii) if the Premises have been damaged or destroyed that they have been fully restored and

(iii) the Premises are fit for and capable of immediate and full occupation and use and

(iv) no work has been carried out to the Premises by the Tenant which has diminished the rental value of the Premises and

there being disregarded (so far as may be permitted by law)

(i) any effect on rent of the fact that the Tenant has been in occupation of the Premises and

(ii) any goodwill attached or attributable to the Premises by reason of any trade or business carried on by the Tenant and

(iii) any increase in rental value attributable to improvements (shown to be such by the Tenant) made to the Premises by and at the expense of the Tenant within the period of 21 years prior to the Relevant Review Date with the prior written consent of the Landlord other than in pursuance of an obligation on the part of the Tenant and

(iv) any Enactment restricting the amount of the yearly rent which the Landlord may lawfully demand or receive or which the Tenant may lawfully pay

(c) The expression "the Referee" shall mean an independent Chartered Surveyor experienced in the letting and valuation of property used for the Permitted Use who shall be appointed either by agreement between the parties by a date one month prior to the Relevant Review Date or one month after such date as the parties may agree under sub-clause (4) of this clause whichever shall be the later or in the absence of such agreement on the application of either party by the President for the time being of the Royal Institution of Chartered Surveyors or some other officer of that body if the President be unable to act

(2) Before on or after the Review Date or each of the Review Dates the Rent shall be reviewed and the Rent in respect of the Relevant Review Period shall be either the Rent payable immediately prior to the Relevant Review Date or the Market Rent whichever shall be the higher

(3) If for any reason whatever the Rent in respect of the Relevant Review Period shall not have been ascertained by the date of its commencement then

(a) The Tenant shall pay on account rent at the rate payable immediately prior to the Relevant Review Date until the Rent in respect of the Relevant Review Period shall have been ascertained and

b) If following such ascertainment the Rent in respect of the Relevant Review Period shall be greater than the Rent payable immediately prior to the Relevant Review Date the Tenant will within 7 days after ascertainment of the Rent in respect of the Relevant Review Period pay to the Landlord a sum equivalent to the Rent in respect of the Relevant Review Period as so ascertained from the commencement thereof to the next usual quarter day after the date of such ascertainment less all sums so paid on account together with interest at the rate of £2.00 per cent above National Westminster Bank PLC base rate from time to time on such sum from the Relevant Review Date until the date of actual payment or the date 21 days after the Rent in respect of the Relevant Review Period shall have been ascertained whichever shall be the earlier together with any further interest payable under clause 5 (3) of this lease

(4) The amount of the Market Rent at the Relevant Review Date shall in default of agreement between the Landlord and the Tenant by a date two months prior to the Relevant Review Date (or such later date as they may agree) be determined by the Referee who shall act as an expert and not as an arbitrator

(5) In addition to the determination of the Market Rent the award of the Referee may also contain directions as to the share in which the expense of the determination (including the expense of the appointment of the Referee) shall be borne and if such award shall contain such directions then such expense shall be borne in such shares but otherwise such expense shall be borne by the Landlord and the Tenant in equal shares and the Landlord and the Tenant mutually covenant the one

with the other to pay their respective shares of such expense accordingly

(6) The provisions of this clause shall apply notwithstanding any failure of either party to take or any delay by either party in taking any step leading to the agreement or determination of the Market Rent and time shall not be deemed to be of the essence of this clause

(7) (a) If at any time during the Term the amount of the Rent is in any way restricted by any Enactment so as to be irrecoverable in part then the maximum amount

from time to time permitted to be recovered shall be recoverable in lieu of the Rent until such restriction shall cease

(b) As soon as such restriction shall cease the full amount of the Rent shall forthwith become payable and the difference between the full amount of the Rent and the amount recoverable prior to the cessation of such restriction proportionate to the period from such cessation to the next subsequent quarter day shall be payable within seven days of such cessation

(c) Within seven days of such cessation the Tenant will pay to the Landlord so far as permitted by law the difference between the Rent and the amount actually paid by the Tenant while such restriction was in force

THE SCHEDULE

PART I

Circumstances in which the Landlord's consent for an assignment of the Premises by the Tenant may be withheld

1. That there are outstanding unpaid monies due from the Tenant to the Landlord under this lease or any deed supplemental to this lease

2. That there is (in the reasonable opinion of the Landlord) a material outstanding breach of the covenants on the part of the Tenant contained in this lease

PART 2

Conditions subject to which the Landlord's consent for an assignment of the Premises by the Tenant may be granted

1. That on or before the assignment the Tenant enters into an agreement with the Landlord under which the Tenant:-

(a) guarantees the performance by the proposed assignee only whilst the assignee is the lessee under this lease of all the covenants on the part of the Tenant contained in this lease

(b) is liable to the Landlord as a principal debtor only whilst the assignee is the lessee under this lease and is not released even if the Landlord gives the proposed assignee extra time to comply with any obligation arising under this lease or does not insist on its strict terms and

(c) agrees that in the event that this lease is disclaimed the Tenant will accept the grant of a new tenancy of the Premises for a term expiring on the date on which the Term would have expired if this lease had not been disclaimed and on the same terms and conditions as the terms and conditions of this Lease at the date of disclaimer

PROVIDED that such agreement shall not impose on the Tenant any liability in relation to any time after the proposed assignee is released from the covenants on the part of the Tenant contained in this lease by virtue of the Landlord and Tenant (Covenants) Act 1995

2. That in the case of an assignment to a private limited company at least two of its directors officers or members or other persons of satisfactory standing to be approved by the Landlord (such approval not to be unreasonably withheld) shall covenant with the Landlord in such document and form as the Landlord shall reasonably require as principal debtors and so that they shall not be released even if the Landlord gives the company extra time to comply with any obligation arising under this lease or does not insist on its strict terms that

(a) the company will pay the Rent and observe and perform the covenants on the part of the Tenant contained in this lease

(b) they will indemnify the Landlord against any loss resulting from a default by the company and

(c) if this lease is disclaimed on the insolvency of the company they will if the Landlord so requires jointly take a new lease of the Premises at the expense of such person on the same terms and conditions as the terms and condition of this lease at the date of the disclaimer for a term equal to the remainder of the term unexpired at such date

SIGNED AND DELIVERED)
)
)

REPAIRS - THE SCHEDULE

Main Roof Externally:

1. The flat crown roof to the main roof structure is covered by felt and chippings and in good order. The mansard slate roof slopes have been re- slated and are in good order.

2. The asphalt valley gutter has been repaired and is in good order.

Back Addition Lean-To Roof Slope:

3. The back addition lean—to roof slope has been re-slated and is in good order.

Asphalt Roof over Shop Area:

4. The asphalt roof has been repaired, minor ridging visible.

External Main Walls:

5. New steel restraining straps (2 no.) fixed to front elevation around bay window structure.

6. Cracking in the rear elevation above the lean—to roof slope has been cut out and repaired.

7. Render repairs made to side elevation at ground level where former opening existed.

8. Portico over Baker Street entrance repaired and in sound condition.

9. Cracking to the end of the shop front at parapet level to Baker Street side repaired.

Rainwater Goods:

10. All rainwater goods replaced with PVC guttering and downpipes.

Chimney Stack:

11.. Defective rendering to chimney stack hacked off and repaired.

External Joinery:

12. New shop front window frames installed.
13. New Shop entrance door and frame installed.
14. Windows to all elevations in reasonable condition.

External Decorations:

15. External decorations are in good order.

INTERNALLY:

Second Floor West Bedroom:

16. The ceilings and walls in good order. Redecorated.
17. Skirtings, architraves and doors in reasonable condition. Paintwork in good order.

Second Floor East Facing Bedroom:

18. Ceilings and walls in good order. Redecorated.
19. Skirtings, architraves and doors paintwork in good order.

Bathroom:

20. Ceilings and walls in good order. Glazed tiling in fair condition.

21. New gas water heater fitted.

22. Sanitaryware reasonable.

23. Ceiling, walls and joinery redecorated.

Staircase:

24. Ceilings and walls redecorated and in good order. Minor defects to lining papers beneath the decorations.

First Floor Main East Room:

25. Ceiling and walls in good order. Redecorated.

26. Skirting, architraves and door in fair condition, repainted.

Kitchen:

27. Ceiling and walls in good order, redecorated.

28. A new sink unit, base unit with worktop and two double cupboard wall units fitted.

29. Glazed tiled splashback in good order.

30. Skirtings, architraves and door in good order, repainted.

<u>W.C.</u>

31 . Ceilings and walls in good order. Redecorated.

32. New W.C. installed.

<u>Ground Floor South Entrance Lobby</u>:

33. Ceiling and walls in reasonable condition, redecorated.

34. Front door repaired, redecorated, fair condition.

35. Doors to basement, staircase and shop in good order, skirtings, architraves reasonable. All joinery repainted.

<u>Back Addition Ground Floor Main Room</u>:

36. **C**eiling fair, **walls repaired.** Basic condition, no decorations.

<u>Rear Passage, Store</u> <u>and</u> **<u>W.C</u>**.

37. Ceiling repaired, walls repaired, basic condition, no decoration.

<u>Cloakroom</u>.

38. ceiling repaired, walls repaired, fair condition, no decoration.

39. Sanitaryware reasonable.

<u>Electrics</u>:

40. Property rewired, in good order.

<u>Shop</u>:

41.. Shop ceiling, walls in good order.
42. Decorations in good order.